Manna gum (*Eucalyptus viminalis*), one of the popular street and roadside trees of southern California. The upright form and the graceful, frond-like branches add a touch of beauty to the landscape.

WESTERN FOREST TREES

*A Guide to the Identification of Trees
and Woods for Students, Teachers,
Farmers and Woodsmen*

by James Berthold Berry

*Illustrated from Photographs
and with Drawings by*
MARY E. EATON

*With a new preface and appendix
with bibliography by*
WOODBRIDGE METCALF

Dover Publications, Inc., New York

Published in Canada by General Publishing Company, Ltd., 30 Lesmill Road, Don Mills, Toronto, Ontario.
Published in the United Kingdom by Constable and Company, Ltd., 10 Orange Street, London WC 2.

This Dover edition, first published in 1964, and reissued in 1966, with a new preface and appendix with bibliography by Woodbridge Metcalf, is a corrected republication of the work originally published by the World Book Company in 1924.

International Standard Book Number: 0-486-21138-X
Library of Congress Catalog Card Number: 64-15497

Manufactured in the United States of America
Dover Publications, Inc.
180 Varick Street
New York, N. Y. 10014

PREFACE TO THE DOVER EDITION

THIS little manual was first issued in 1924 and was intended by Professor Berry to assist school children, farmers and travellers in the eleven western states in becoming more familiar with the important trees of this region and the woods which they produce for lumber, posts, poles and other forest products. It has served well for over forty years in presenting in relatively simple, non-technical terms an introduction to the trees of this vast area, which contains some of the largest, oldest and finest forest trees of the world. A total of 74 trees are described and illustrated, 32 being conifers or "softwoods" and 42 being broadleaf or "hardwoods." Most of these trees have maintained their commercial importance throughout the years, and a number of others have become of value with the increase in population, improvement in highways, access roads and other means of transportation, and in the advance of knowledge and improved technology which enables us to utilize trees for many products unknown in 1924.

Botanical and dendrological knowledge has also advanced materially during these years, and the literature has been enriched by a great number of tree books. Field studies and exploration have also added much to our understanding of the distribution of trees and their reaction to differing soils and climatic conditions throughout the west. Through such studies, mountain species like the Bristlecone Pine, *Pinus aristata*, have been given increased significance because of their great age and persistence under rigorous sub-alpine conditions. Other tree species have achieved importance as ornamentals in parks, gardens and estates, and many exotic species have been imported for use as Christmas trees, windbreaks and minor forest products, and as shade and ornamental trees.

Tree names. Tree names have been a problem throughout the years because of historical factors and the failure of botanists in different areas of the world to agree on a uniform standard. Common names which are well understood in some localities are often applied to entirely different trees in others, and even many Latin scientific names considered to be standard and applied to important tree species for many years, have been changed during the last quarter century to comply with certain rules of botanical precedence. The names used in this manual have been subject to such change in certain cases, and these are pointed out in the appendix. In general, the names in most common use are indicated in the *Check List of Native and Naturalized Trees of the United States* by Elbert L. Little Jr., Agriculture Handbook No. 41, Forest Service, U. S. D. A., Washington D. C., 1953. This is also the best reference in which to check the range of each species and variety as determined by recent field observation.

Examples of the somewhat confusing use of common names in this volume may be cited as follows: on page 84 the name "true cedars" is used for the two species of the genus *Chamaecyparis* which are now usually designated as "false cypresses"; the name "true cedar" is now applied to three species of the genus

Cedrus. These exotic trees—Deodar Cedar, *Cedrus deodara* from the Himalayas, Atlas Cedar, *Cedrus atlantica* from the Atlas Mountains of North Africa and Lebanon Cedar, *Cedrus libanensis* from Lebanon and Turkey—are extensively planted as ornamentals along the Pacific Coast. On page 208 the name "manzanita" is used for the Texas Madrone, now designated in the *Check List* as *Arbutus texana,* whereas the numerous shrubs of the genus *Arctostaphylos,* widely distributed in foothill chaparral cover, are now universally known as manzanitas. On page 54 the name "red fir" should not be applied to the Western Larch, *Larix occidentalis,* and on page 66 the term "larch" is not valid as applied to Noble Fir, *Abies procera,* formerly known as *Abies nobilis.*

Aids in tree identification. While this small volume will serve as a very good introduction to the study of western trees, it should be supplemented by some of the reference books listed in the Bibliography. In many states the local forestry departments have issued pocket manuals which will help greatly in determining the range and characteristics of trees within their borders. Botany teachers in local high schools, junior colleges or state universities may be consulted and the county farm advisor, extension forester or extension horticulturist from the Agricultural Extension Service may also be helpful. Rangers of the U. S. Forest Service, National Park Service or the State Department of Natural Resources or Conservation are often available for similar help. However, the use of exotic trees in ornamental plantings in cities, towns and settled areas has

become so common as to be a very important considera-
tion. Here local arborists, ornamental horticulturists
and members of the International Shade Tree Conference may assist in identification. This organization
has issued (August 1965) a bulletin entitled *Shade
Tree Evaluation,* which lists for various regions of the
United States the preferred shade tree species, and
under each four or more classes as to desirability for
the region. Such lists naturally include most of the
exotic tree species which have been successfully introduced in these areas.

Arboreta or tree collections. In a number of places
it is possible to visit collections of planted trees in city
parks, college campuses or arboreta where many of
the trees are labeled. Some areas of this kind are:

University of Washington Arboretum, Seattle, Washing-
   ton
City Parks, Portland, Oregon
Strybing Arboretum and Golden Gate Park, San Francisco,
   California
Los Angeles State and County Arboretum, Arcadia, Cali-
   fornia
University of California campus plantings, Berkeley,
   Davis, Los Angeles, California
Capitol Park, Sacramento, California
Roeding Park, Fresno, California
Institute of Forest Genetics, Placerville, California
   (Pines)

Introduced species. This manual discusses only four
species not native to the western region: the Black
Locust from the Middle Western United States (p.
119), and three species of Eucalyptus from Australia

(p. 190). The locust is widely naturalized over much of western America, but the eucalypts will grow only in relatively mild climatic areas of coastal and valley California where many other species of this interesting genus are in common use as ornamentals. These eucalypts have indeed "transformed the face of California," as one writer recently put it, but most of the plantations set out about the turn of the century have been removed, where the land under irrigation proved to be more valuable for other crops. The wood of these fast-growing young trees was of inferior quality for lumber, but in recent years it has been successfully used in the manufacture of pulp and particle-board products, and experimental planting of several species is being carried on in favorable cut-over areas in the north coast section of California. A number of eucalypts with showy flowers or attractive foliage are in common use as ornamentals. Other exotic trees are far too numerous to be dealt with in this volume, with the exception of a few conifers being grown in plantations as Christmas trees. A few hardy species have escaped from cultivation and are occasionally found growing in the wild. Among these are the following: Chinese Tree of Heaven, *Ailanthus altissima,* European Silver Poplar, *Populus alba,* Myrobalan Plum, *Prunus ceracifera,* Apple, *Malus pumila* (in Washington and Idaho), Siberian Elm, *Ulmus pumila,* Rock or Cork Elm, *Ulmus thomasi,* American Elm, *Ulmus americana,* Weeping Willow, *Salix babylonica,* English Hawthorn, *Crataegus oxycantha,* and in mild climatic areas, Blackwood Acacia, *Acacia melanoxylon.* Some other species may occasionally become established along stream banks or adjacent to irrigated fields. A more complete list of introduced species will be found in the appendix.

Berkeley, California   WOODBRIDGE METCALF
January, 1966

PREFACE TO THE FIRST EDITION

TREES are man's greatest friends. They supply him with food and shelter; they conserve water power and preserve the soil; they soften the climate for God's creatures; they inspire holy and beautiful thoughts. Without trees the land becomes inhospitable and unkind, and civilization disintegrates. No greater lesson can be taught by our schools than the creation of a personal, growing affection for our tree friends.

The subject of tree and wood identification may be introduced into our public school curriculum at any time after the fourth grade. Surely every high school graduate should be able to recognize all the important trees which occur locally and to speak intelligently of the character and uses of the wood. In connection with the study of birds and other phases of nature study, the identification of trees should be made a part of every field trip. Pupils should be encouraged to bring leaves and twigs from home in the identification of all trees on the home grounds. A portion of the school planting may well consist of a small tree garden for use in connection with this subject.

The success of laboratory and class exercises in tree identification is contingent upon the presence of an abundant supply of teaching materials, such as leaves, buds, sections of bark, and wood specimens. Each pupil should be required to make up an herbarium of the leaves and twigs of common trees, using a loose-leaf notebook with unruled pages. Needless to say, each specimen should be carefully pressed and thoroughly dried before being mounted.   After it has been mounted, the specimen should be neatly labeled.

Bark and wood characteristics may be studied from small sections of stems or branches 2 to 4 inches in diameter and of convenient length.   A thin slab taken from the block will show the "bastard" grain; and a cut from one end of the block to the other, through the center, will show the "quarter" grain.   Each pupil may be required to make up such a collection for the trees of the community.   The cutting and smoothing of the wood will give some knowledge of its hardness.

In determining the name of a species, the student may be puzzled by the inconsistency of the common names. Sometimes several names are applied to one species. These names vary according to the region, and even within the same region. Furthermore, the common name is often meaningless, and usually is not descriptive. It is for this reason that botanists have adopted "scientific" (Latin) names for the trees.   The scientific name is accepted by botanists the world over as the one authentic name.   Once a tree has been "run down" in the key, the name should be referred to in the index to locate the page upon which the description occurs.

The illustrations used in this book as an aid to the identification of the various species have been so planned that wherever possible the figures are shown in natural size.   The line which accompanies each illustration represents one inch.   When this line appears a full inch long, it will be understood that the figures are natural size; when less or more than an inch, the figures are proportionally reduced or enlarged.

The Western forest, comprising the Rocky Mountain and Pacific Coast regions, is mostly of a coniferous nature; the hardwoods are of minor importance. Because of the uneven topography, the region varies widely in climatic conditions. Areas of productive farm land and forest land are interspersed with unproductive semi-desert territory. In general, the western slopes and mountain tops receive an abundant precipitation, while the interior valleys and eastern slopes are characterized by periods of drought and a low annual precipitation. The growing season and mean temperature are affected by the altitude of the region; the more or less semi-tropical temperatures of the lower elevations in the southern part of the region give way gradually with increasing altitude to arctic temperatures and perpetual snow. The temperate-climate trees which occur at sea level in the northern part of the region are found at elevations of from 6000 to 10,000 feet in the southern part. In the study of the distribution of forest trees, one must therefore consider altitude quite as much as latitude. Not infrequently one may traverse several "tree zones" in the course of a day's travel into the mountains.

A large portion of the forest area of the region, particularly that which occurs at higher elevations, is included within the boundaries of the National Forests and is under systematic regulation; this insures to the industries a steady and uniform supply of forest products. Stockmen and ranchers do not feel the same need for producing supplies of wood for home use that stimulates the farmer of the East to retain and care for a piece of woodland as part of the farm operation. Nevertheless tree

growth is essential to the protection of orchards and vine-
yards, and the planting of shade trees, roadside trees, and
ornamental trees about the farmstead is as important as
in other sections of the country.   The rancher and stock-
man should have a knowledge of the trees suitable for
windbreak planting, and it is equally important that he
know the trees of the National Forest from which he
draws his supplies of fuel and farm timbers.   This
knowledge is of special value in those cases where the
user is given the privilege of selecting the material to
be removed under his "free use" permit.   Because of
the limited supply of suitable hardwood material, it is
often advisable for the rancher to grow the wood needed
for farm repairs, such as eveners, singletrees, ax and
tool handles, etc.   In the semi-desert regions where the
trees may be irrigated until they become well established,
it is a practice to plant Eastern trees which have succeeded
under the prairie conditions of the Middle West.   Plantations of black locust have thus yielded as great a labor
income as farm enterprises of a more intensive nature.

The author desires to express his grateful appreciation
of the many kindnesses extended by the members of the
United States Forest Service during the preparation of
this handbook.   Most of the illustrations used are taken
from the publication of the United States Department of
Agriculture entitled "Forest Trees of the Pacific Slope,"
with the consent and approval of the Forest Service.

CONTENTS

INTRODUCTORY

PART I. THE NEEDLE-LEAF TREES

Section 1. Trees with Needle-like Leaves:

Section 2. Trees with Scale-like Leaves:

PART II. THE BROADLEAF TREES

Section 1. Trees with Compound Leaves:

xv

Contents

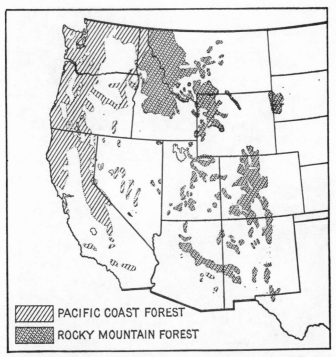

PACIFIC COAST FOREST
ROCKY MOUNTAIN FOREST

FIG. 1. Map showing the geographic area covered by this Manual. The text is limited to a discussion of the commercially important forest trees of the western United States, which belong to two separate forest regions: (1) the Pacific Coast forest and (2) the Rocky Mountain forest. Altitude is an important factor of climate in the West and trees tend to be distributed in horizontal zones. For example, the altitudinal distribution of a given tree may be from sea level to 3000 feet in the northern section and from 6000 to 9000 feet in the southern section. Precipitation is affected by the direction of the prevailing winds, which in the West are from the southwest. This explains the dense growth on the western slopes and the often semi-arid conditions of the eastern slopes.

FIG. 2. The wide-spreading form of the blue gum (*Eucalyptus globulus*).

INTRODUCTORY

A. HOW TO IDENTIFY TREES

The trees are divided, by lumbermen, into two groups — the " softwoods " and the " hardwoods." In early days the former term was applied principally to the white pine and the latter to white oak. At present, however, each group includes woods of both hard and soft texture. The botanical terms " evergreen " and " deciduous " are nearly as inexact, since some of the trees of each group drop their leaves at the end of the growing season, while others retain their leaves for more than a single season. From the standpoint of the woodsman, the terms " needle-leaf " and " broadleaf " are much more definite, the needle-leaf group including both needle-like and scale-like leaves (the pines and their allies) and the broadleaf group comprising the so-called " hardwoods," or deciduous trees.

Each kind of tree (species) possesses certain definite characteristics by which it may be distinguished from others. The characteristics most easily observed are those of form, bark, foliage, branching, leaf, and bud.

Form. Grown in the open, each kind of tree develops a form or shape which, for that particular tree, is characteristic. Form varies with the age and with competition (density of stand). Some kinds develop a pyramidal crown when young, and an open, flat crown when old. Others, again, develop an irregular crown in youth, and a broadly rounded or oblong crown in later life. Under conditions of competition the " light-demanding " (intolerant) trees develop a long, clear stem and an

FIG. 3.   The rounded form of the Oregon maple (*Acer macrophyllum*).

irregular or flattened crown, while the " shade-endur-
ing " (tolerant) kinds retain their branches for a long
period of time.   In some kinds the stem breaks up into
a number of large branches, while in others the stem
remains undivided.   The cedars, firs, and spruces, in the
youthful stage at least, are recognized by the pyramidal
form, which differs markedly from the irregular form
of the pines.   The valley oak and tanbark oak develop
broadly rounded crowns of irregular branches, the spread
of crown often being greater than the total height.
The crown of the eucalyptus is rather irregular in out-

U.S. Forest Service
FIG. 4. The pyramidal form of the white fir (*Abies concolor*).

line, due to the development of a few large branches which, however, present a most graceful appearance. The maple and alder throw off many comparatively small branches along the stem, the crown developing into a full, rounded, and dense mass. Madroña, on the other hand, " sheds " the lower branches, producing an open, irregular, rather scraggly form. The tolerant kinds, such as spruce, fir, cedar, and laurel, retain the lower branches even in dense shade, preserving the form of youth for many years. The intolerant trees, in contrast, quickly " shade out " the lower branches; this

University of California

FIG. 5. The irregular form of the sugar pine (*Pinus lambertiana*).

results in a " clear " stem and an irregular, open crown. Form is also influenced by the character of twigs, the few, coarse twigs of the pine, walnut, ash, and elder forming an open crown, and the numerous, fine twigs of the birch, laurel, and cypress producing a dense crown.

Bark. Great variation exists in the bark characteristics of the different kinds of trees, not only as regards texture, hardness, thickness, and surface, but also in respect to taste, odor, and color. The two most noticeable characteristics are those of color and surface configuration. One may readily recognize the blue gum by the thin, smooth, bluish-green bark; the madroña and birch by the papery, scurfy bark; the juniper and incense cedar by the soft, fibrous, spirally twisted bark; the

FIG. 6. The broadly conical form of the Monterey cypress (*Cupressus macrocarpa*). The numerous fine twigs give the crown a dense, closely compact appearance.

yellow pine by the orange-colored, scaly plates, separated by shallow fissures; and the sugar pine and Douglas fir by the brown, prominently ridged bark. The trees with a thick bark show a pronounced ridging, separated by deep fissures; the ridges are either broad, as in sugar pine and the redwood, or narrow, as in the maple and ash. On the other hand, the trees with a thin bark seldom show a pronounced ridging, but appear smooth, as in the gums; scurfy, as in the madroña and birch; broken into small plates, as in the dogwood; or scaly,

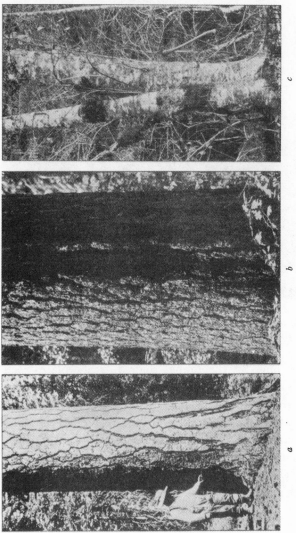

FIGS. 7, 8, and 9. Types of bark forms: *a*, plated (yellow pine); *b*, scaly, ridged (sugar pine); *c*, smooth, lichen-covered (red alder). (*Photographs a and c from U. S. Forest Service, b from University of California.*)

FIGS. 10, 11, and 12. Types of bark forms: *d*, flaking (blue gum); *e*, stringy, ridged (redwood); *f*, hard, broadly ridged (tanbark oak). (*Photographs d and e from U. S. Forest Service, f from American Forestry Magazine.*)

as in the lodgepole pine. The character of the bark on branches and small stems is also a means of identification, the bark becoming roughened and scaly or ridged even on small branches, as in the yellow pine and the white oaks, or remaining smooth until the branches are several inches in diameter, as in the white pine, the sugar pine, the firs, the live oaks, the maple, and the alder. The bark and twigs of laurel, the willows, the cottonwoods, and the eucalyptus possess a distinctive odor and taste, which is characteristic of these trees.

Foliage. Aside from the shape of the leaf, the foliage of some trees possesses definite characteristics which serve to identify them. The feathery clusters of pine needles and the stiff, blue-green foliage of the fir may be recognized at a considerable distance. Quite as noticeable is the dark, glossy foliage of the laurel, the deep green of the white oaks, the yellow-green of the black oaks, the lead-green of the mountain mahogany, the light green of the ash, and the metallic luster of the foliage on the gums. The cottonwoods and a few of the oaks produce leaves on the previous year's growth only, presenting a very different appearance from those trees which develop leaves for some distance along the branches. The tolerant [1] and intolerant [1] trees may be distinguished by the density of the foliage.

Branching. The branching may be opposite or alternate, at a wide angle with the branch ·or stem, as in the maple, the cottonwood, the pines, and the spruces; or at a narrow angle, as in the gums, the birches, and the ash. Those trees which produce buds arranged op-

[1] Of shade.

posite on the twigs usually show a distinctive branching in the same order, as in the maple and ash. Some of the needle-leaf trees, notably the firs, spruces, and white pines, show distinct whorls of branches at intervals along the stem. Others show no distinct order of branching, as the cedars, the yew, the redwood, and the majority of the broadleaf trees. The type of branching, when considered in connection with form and foliage, serves as a useful means of identification when one is at a distance.

Leaves. The shape of a leaf, as well as the color and texture, is a positive means of identification and one which is depended upon most generally by students. In the needle-leaf group the pines are distinguished from their allies (firs, spruces, hemlock, Douglas fir, etc.) by the " bundling " of the needles, from two to five (except the single-leaf pine, *Pinus monophylla*) being bound together at the base and each needle in cross-section forming a portion of a circle. The greater the number of needles in a bundle and the longer the needles, the more " feathery " the tree in appearance. The leaves of the larch occur in groups of fifteen to twenty-five as " fascicles " but with no " bundling," as in the pines. Again, the leaves may be set on small, raised points of the bark, as in the spruces. In some cases the leaves are arranged on two sides of the twig (two-ranked), as in hemlock, while in other cases the needles are scattered spirally about the twig, as in the firs and spruces. The scale-like leaves also differ noticeably among themselves, the leaves of the Port Orford cedar being arranged " opposite " while those of the junipers are in threes about the twig. The needles, both needle-like and scale-like, may be harsh (stiff and sharp) to the touch, as in the spruces, the yew, and the junipers; or soft (blunt-pointed and flexible), as in the firs, hemlock, redwood, and Douglas fir. In the needle-leaf group the larch is the only tree which is deciduous.

Leaf forms are even more varied in the broadleaf group of trees, but the characteristic is of value during the growing season only, since most of the trees of this group are deciduous. Two general forms are recognized — the simple leaf, which consists of but a single " blade," and the compound leaf, consisting of a number of leaflets attached to a central " leaf " stem. The simple leaves are further classified on a basis of indentation (lobed or divided) and margin (toothed or entire). The leaf of the white or black oak is lobed; that of the maple is divided; those of the alder, cherry, and tanbark oak are toothed; and that of the eucalyptus is entire. The compound leaves are divided into two groups: the " pinnately" compound, as in the ash and walnut; and the " palmately" compound, as in the buckeye.

The leaves and twigs of many trees possess a distinctive taste and odor, which may serve as means of identification, as in the laurel, the cottonwood, the willow, the birch, the cherry, and the gums.

Buds. Buds and twig characteristics serve as useful means of knowing the trees during the dormant season, when most of the broadleaf trees, and some of the needle-leaf trees, are without foliage. Buds may be arranged oppositely on the twig, as in maple and ash; or alternately, as in the oaks, the cottonwood, and the gums.

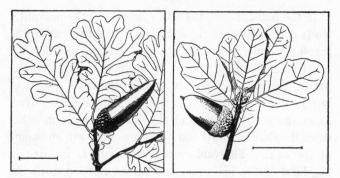

FIGS. 13 and 14. Branches of California white oak (left) and rock oak (right), showing how the leaves, fruit, and buds help in identifying closely related species. A careful examination and comparison of the two drawings will reveal many differences in the size, shape, and quality of the parts shown.

Occasionally they occur in threes about the twig, as in the juniper. They may be scaly (tender minute leaves and inflorescence covered with protective woody scales), as in the maple, the ash, and the cottonwood; or naked (the outer leaves of the bud forming a protective covering over the tender tissues within), as in the walnuts. The winter bud may be full, large, and covered with many scales, as in the buckeye and cottonwood; or small and covered with but a few scales, as in the birch, the alder, and the oaks; or the entire bud may be inclosed in one scale, as in the willow. A false terminal bud produces a zigzag growth of the twig, as in the sycamore; while a true terminal bud produces a straight twig, as in the maple. There may be a single bud at one point on the twig, as in the ash; or one or two smaller buds beside the main bud, as in the maple. Again, the bud may be buried in the wood (submerged), as in the black locust, the screw bean, and the mesquite. Buds may be spaced regularly along the twig, as in the maple, the cherry, and the gums; or they may be clustered at the ends of the twigs, as in the oaks. In the needle-leaf group the buds usually occur in whorls of two to five. In some cases the buds are sharp-pointed, as in the cottonwoods and the cherry; while in other cases they are rounded and blunt, as in the ash and some of the oaks. The bud of the sycamore is inclosed in the base of the leaf stem and is not noticed until the leaves fall.

The color of the pith of the twig varies from brown, as in walnut, to white, as in cottonwood. In some trees the pith is formed in thin " plates," as in the walnut and the hackberry, while in other trees it is solid, as in the willow and the sycamore. The pith may be large in cross-section, as in the elder; or very small, as in the mahogany. Again, the pith may be star-shaped in cross-section, as in the oaks; or circular, as in the cottonwood.

The color of the twig has already been noted as a means of identification. Some twigs are green, some gray, some red-brown, with many variations in between. Another helpful characteristic of the twig is the presence or absence of outgrowths. The locust and screw bean produce thorns which are peculiar to themselves. The willow does not have thorns but produces tiny leaves (stipules) at the base of the leaf stem.

Fruit. Most of the forest trees do not begin to bear seed until they have passed the sapling stage of growth, and the fruit is usually present for but a short season.

But the character of the fruit, when present, is an excellent means of identification. Every boy is familiar with walnuts, cherries, acorns, and pine cones. Less known, but equally characteristic, are the catkin fruits of the cottonwood and willow, the pod fruit of the locust, the valved fruit of the gums, the cherry-like fruits of the dogwood and the bearberry, the plum-like fruit of the madroña and the nutmeg tree, the clusters of slender, winged seeds of the ash, the winged, double seed of the maple, and the peculiar ball-like fruit of the sycamore.

In the needle-leaf group of trees the cones (fruit) are of great assistance in identification. The cones may be cylindrical, as in the sugar pine, the white pine, the hemlock, the firs, and the spruces; broadly pyramidal, as in the yellow pine; or round (globose), as in the cypress and some of the cedars. The cone scales may be thin and papery, as in the hemlock; or hard and bony, as in the digger pine. The scales may be smooth, as in the sugar pine; or armed with sharp-pointed projections, as in the lodgepole pine. The bracts (leaf-like structures between the cone scales) may be excluded (project beyond the scales), as in the Douglas fir and larch (red fir),[1] or included (bracts shorter than cone scales), as in the spruces and most of the firs.

The cones may stand erect on the twigs, as in the firs; or they may hang pendent, as in the spruces. In other cases they are held laterally or pendent, as in the pines.

[1] The larch is often erroneously called "red fir," although in reality it has no connection with the firs.

The color of the immature cone varies from green, as in the spruce, to purple, as in the firs, and brownish, as in the pines. At maturity the cones, in most cases, turn brown (light or dark).

Identification. No one set of characteristics may be depended upon at all seasons of the year, nor for both young and old individuals; rather, a combination of characteristics must be relied upon. During the growing season most attention will be given to the form, foliage, and bark; during the dormant season, to the form, branching, and bark. A more minute study brings in the leaves, when present, and the buds, when the leaves are absent. Certain gross characteristics will classify a tree as a member of a definite group, but one must resort to the more refined characteristics if he desires to name the tree. For example, one may recognize a tree at a considerable distance as a member of the needle-leaf group by the shape and foliage. As he approaches the tree he is able to place it in a more restricted group because of the branching and bark. However, it may be any one of a dozen trees of this group. As he comes nearer he is able to see the fruit and the branching of the twigs. Perhaps he has placed it as a juniper. Now it is necessary for him to come still closer and to examine the leaves and fruit minutely; then he is able to name the tree a " one-seeded juniper."

For purposes of description the trees in this book have been grouped arbitrarily on a basis of leaf form, the various keys being found on the pages listed on the next page.

KEY TO THE TREE GROUPS

References

Bulletin 17, Forest Service, U. S. D. A., " Check List of the Forest Trees of the United States."

Bulletin, University of Nebraska, " A Twig and Bud Key."

Bulletin, University of Nebraska, " Notes on Bark Structure."

" Manual of Trees of North America," Sargent, C. S. (Houghton Mifflin Company, Boston; 1905.)

B. HOW TO IDENTIFY WOODS

Wood is not a uniform (homogeneous) material such as metal but is built up of many small, tube-like and spindle-like elements (cells) which are closely packed together. The largest of these cells are less than one fiftieth of an inch in diameter and a quarter of an inch in length, the only exceptions being the vessels (trachetory elements) in which the end walls have been dissolved away to form long, continuous transportation tubes. The elements which form a basis for wood identification are: tracheids, vessels, wood fibers, medullary rays, and resin ducts.

Tracheids. The tracheids are thin-walled tubes which constitute the larger proportion of the wood of the needle-leaf group of trees. In cross-section the openings of the tracheids are of approximately equal size and shape and are arranged in regular rows across the annual ring. Tracheids occur to but a small extent in the hardwood group of trees.

Vessels. The vessels are continuous tubes with moderately thin walls but surrounded by thick-walled wood fibers. In cross-section the vessels are known as "pores." They occur in the hardwoods only, the needle-leaf woods being known as "nonporous" woods. The vessels are not of the same size in all parts of the ring, the pores of the spring wood being often conspicuously larger.

Wood fibers. Surrounding the vessels, and constituting the greater part of the wood tissue of the broadleaf trees, are thick-walled, tapering cells known as wood

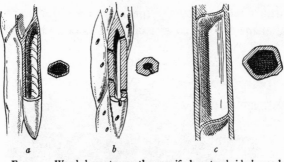

FIG. 15.   Wood elements, greatly magnified: *a*, tracheid; *b*, wood
fiber; *c*, vessel.

fibers. Wood fibers give strength and density to the
wood tissue.

Medullary rays.* Lying at right angles to the axis of
the tree and extending in radial lines from the center
of the tree are thin layers of thin-walled, short, rectangular cells which function as lines of communication between the outer and inner portions of the stem.   When
but a few rows of cells in width they are designated as
" fine " rays; when noticeably wide to the unaided eye,
as " broad " rays.   The fine rays may be visible to the
unaided eye, visible with a hand magnifier only, or invisible except under the microscope.   In the oaks and
the sycamore both broad and fine rays are present; in
the maple, cherry, and alder groups fine rays only are
present, although distinct to the unaided eye; and in
the needle-leaf group extremely fine rays only are present.

* These structures are now more commonly referred to as wood
rays, and this latter term should be understood wherever "medullary rays" appears.

Resin ducts. Properly speaking, resin ducts are not wood elements, but consist of deposits of gum in spaces

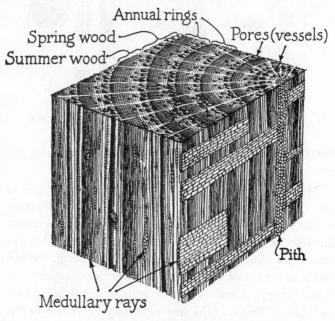

FIG. 16. Section of a hardwood (hickory), showing the structure diagrammatically.

between the wood elements (tracheids). In cross-section they appear as small, irregular spots, dark-colored in the light woods (spring wood), light-colored in the dark woods (summer wood). They appear consistently in certain woods, however, and serve as useful means of identification. In the pine group the resin ducts are numerous, conspicuous, and regularly distributed; in the spruce group, extremely small, but regularly distributed; in Douglas fir, conspicuous, but grouped; and in the larch group rather small and few in number. On surfaced, kiln-dried pine boards the resin ducts appear as short, dark streaks, especially noticeable in sapwood.

Physical properties. In addition to the structural characteristics of wood there are certain physical properties which aid in identification; namely, color, taste, odor, weight, and texture.

Color. The heartwood, as a rule, is quite constant as to color in any particular kind of wood, serving as an indication if not as a means of positive identification. The white and black oaks, the walnuts, and the cedars are readily distinguished by color. A few woods, such as Douglas fir, walnut, and eucalyptus, vary considerably in color of wood, yet the variability within a group is characteristic.

Taste and odor. Certain woods, notably red cedar, nutmeg, the true cedars, juniper, and incense cedar, may be recognized by a characteristic odor and taste. In connection with color and structure these properties serve as a practical means of identification.

Weight. Except in extreme cases weight is not a ready means of identification, since this property varies within rather wide limits according to the rate of growth and the part of the tree. In general, those woods having a specific gravity of more than .50 may be considered " heavy," and those with less than .50 "light." The following may be classed as heavy woods : hickory, oak, nutmeg, ash, eucalyptus, dogwood, yew, Douglas fir, mesquite, and mountain mahogany. Those which are considered light woods are redwood, big tree, the true firs, spruce, hemlock, the true cedars, and white pine.

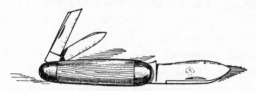

Fig. 17.   Type of pocketknife recommended for use in wood identification.

An intermediate group of moderately heavy woods would include such kinds as black walnut, maple, birch, cherry, hard pine, and juniper.

Texture.   Aside from hardness, which varies quite regularly with weight, it is possible to classify woods according to fineness of grain.   Yew is characteristically fine-grained and redwood is coarse-grained.   Alder, maple, cherry, black walnut, madroña, and the gums are classed with the fine-grained; big tree, red cedar, hemlock, the true firs, and catalpa with the coarse-grained.   Between the two extremes occur all gradations of fineness and coarseness.

Instruments.   But two instruments are necessary in wood identification; namely, the hand magnifier and the pocketknife.   The magnifier should be of ten to twenty diameters, preferably of the " flat field " type. Some of the barrel (Coddington) forms are less expensive and prove satisfactory.   On the farm there arise so many occasions which call for the use of a magnifier (insect and disease work, etc.) that one is warranted in recommending the better type of glass.   The knife should have a large, wide blade of high quality steel, since none but the best grade of material will hold the razor-like edge necessary for "clean" cutting. An oilstone of good quality for keeping the knife sharp should be considered a part of the necessary equipment.

FIG. 18. A Coddington lens, one of the best forms of hand magnifier.

IDENTIFICATION

The broad division of the woods into the porous and non-porous groups will be the most difficult for the beginner. There should be repeated examinations of different woods with the hand magnifier and comparison with the figures [1] illustrating representative woods. The uniform structure of the softwoods is often apparent to the unaided eye, as one becomes familiar with the more common kinds. , A clean-cut cross-section of redwood or white pine (examples of non-porous woods) indicates very characteristically the uniform arrangement of the tracheid openings and the regularity of their diameters. The same uniformity is exhibited in the hard pines, the summer wood being differentiated from the spring wood by the resinous color and a thickening of the walls. The porous woods, on the other hand, are not uniform in structure, a clean cross-section showing the pores of larger diameter irregularly scattered through the annual ring among the wood fibers with their microscopic openings. In many of the woods of this group the pores are quite prominent in cross-section. Par-

[1] Forest Service, Bulletin 10, "Timber."

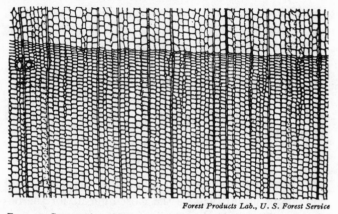

Forest Products Lab., U. S. Forest Service

Fig. 19. Cross-section of Sitka spruce (*Picea sitchensis*), a non-porous wood having little summer wood and small resin ducts.

ticularly is this true of the " ring-porous " woods, which are characterized by one to several rows of comparatively large pores in the spring wood, the pores of the summer wood being much smaller. The "diffuse-porous" woods, in contrast, do not show any marked difference in the size of the pores in spring and summer wood; nor are the pores often large enough to be discernible to the unaided eye. Between the two groups, ring-porous and diffuse-porous, are several woods with intermediate types of structure (walnuts, for example), the pores being somewhat larger in the spring wood and gradually grading off into the summer wood.

Key to the Woods (Use with Hand Lens)

I. NON–POROUS WOODS

A. Summer wood pronounced, annual rings very distinct
1. Resin ducts present, conspicuous
   a. Resin ducts uniformly distributed

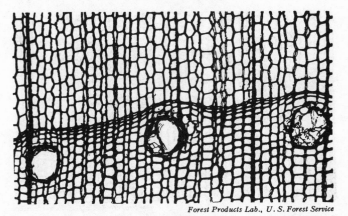

Forest Products Lab., U. S. Forest Service

FIG. 20. Cross-section of sugar pine (*Pinus lambertiana*), a non-porous wood, showing the very large resin ducts.

(1) Heartwood yellow-brown . . . . JEFFREY PINE
(2) Heartwood red-brown . . . . . YELLOW PINE
   b. Resin ducts grouped
(1) Heartwood red-brown . . . . . . DOUGLAS FIR

B. Summer wood present, grades into spring wood, annual rings distinct
  1. RESIN DUCTS PRESENT, SMALL
     a. Heartwood red-brown . . . . LARCH
  2. RESIN DUCTS ABSENT
     a. Wood with pronounced odor
       (1) Wood heavy, heartwood yellow . . . . . NUTMEG
       (2) Wood light, heartwood red-brown . . RED CEDAR
     b. Wood without pronounced odor
       (1) Wood heavy, dense
         (*a*) Heartwood orange . . . . YEW
       (2) Wood light, coarse-grained
         (*a*) Heartwood light red-brown . . . . HEMLOCK
         (*b*) Heartwood red to maroon . . . . REDWOOD

C. Summer wood absent or very limited, annual rings rather indistinct
  1. RESIN DUCTS PRESENT
     a. Resin ducts conspicuous, numerous
       (1) Grain fine, ducts noticeable . . . . WHITE PINE

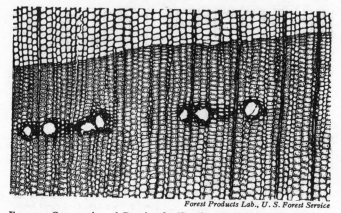

Forest Products Lab., U. S. Forest Service

FIG. 21. Cross-section of Douglas fir (*Pseudotsuga taxifolia*), a non-porous wood, showing pronounced summer wood and grouped resin ducts.

      (2) Grain coarse, ducts very large . . . SUGAR PINE
  b. Resin ducts inconspicuous, few
      (1) Heartwood pale yellow . . . ENGELMANN SPRUCE
      (2) Heartwood reddish . . . . SITKA SPRUCE
  2. RESIN DUCTS ABSENT
    a. Wood with pronounced odor
      (1) Heartwood pale yellow . . . . . YELLOW CEDAR
      (2) Heartwood yellow to brown . PORT ORFORD CEDAR
      (3) Heartwood pale red-brown . . . INCENSE CEDAR
    b. Wood odorless
      (1) Grain fine, heavy
        (*a*) Heartwood red-brown . . . . . . JUNIPER
        (*b*) Heartwood light brown . . . . . . CYPRESS'
      (2) Grain coarse, light
        (*a*) Heartwood pale brown . . . . . WHITE FIR
        (*b*) Heartwood reddish . . . . RED FIR

II. POROUS WOODS (1)

Ring-porous woods (noticeably large
pores in spring wood)

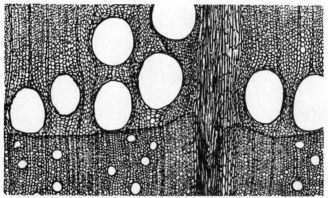

Forest Products Lab., U.S. Forest Service

FIG. 22.   Cross-section of red oak (*Quercus rubra*), a ring-porous wood, showing the large pores of the spring wood and a section of a medullary ray.   (This is an Eastern species, but it closely resembles California black oak (*Q. californica*) in structure.)

A. Sharp break between spring wood and summer wood

      1. BROAD MEDULLARY RAYS PRESENT
          a. Heartwood light brown . . . . VALLEY OAK
          b. Heartwood reddish brown . . . . . . .BLACK OAK
      2. BROAD MEDULLARY RAYS ABSENT
          a. Single row of large pores in spring wood
             (1) Wood heavy, hard, dense . . . . . . HICKORY
          b. Several rows of large pores in spring wood
             (1) Wood heavy, dense
                (*a*) Wood light in color
                    i. Heartwood light brown . . . . . . ASH
                (*b*) Wood dark in color
                    i. Heartwood greenish brown . . . . LOCUST
                    ii. Heartwood dark red . . . . . MESQUITE

III. POROUS WOODS (2)

Intermediate woods (not distinctly
ring porous)

A. Pores distinct, grading off into summer wood   . . . WALNUT

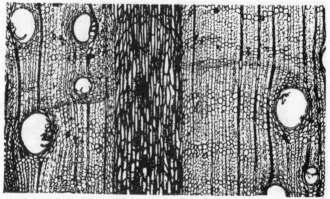

Forest Products Lab., U. S. Forest Service

FIG. 23.   Cross-section of tanbark oak (*Quercus densiflora*), a ring-porous wood, showing scattered pores and a portion of a broad medullary ray.

IV. POROUS WOODS (3)

Diffuse-porous woods (pores of same size throughout annual ring)

A. Broad medullary rays present

    1. HEARTWOOD REDDISH BROWN . . . . SYCAMORE
    2. HEARTWOOD BROWNISH . . . . .TANBARK OAK
    3. HEARTWOOD REDDISH . . . . LIVE OAK

B. Broad medullary rays absent

    1. WOOD HEAVY, DENSE
       a. Heartwood light color
          (1) Medullary rays indistinct
             (*a*) Heartwood yellowish or brownish .   EUCALYPTUS
             (*b*) Heartwood light red . . . . LAUREL
             (*c*) Heartwood dark brown . . . . . MADROÑA
          (2) Medullary rays distinct
             (*a*) Heartwood red-brown . . . . . . CHERRY
             (*b*) Heartwood light brown, bright . . . MAPLE
             (*c*) Heartwood brownish, dull . . . . . ALDER
    2. WOOD LIGHT, BRITTLE, POROUS
       a. Heartwood brownish, dull . . . . . . COTTONWOOD
       b. Heartwood dirty white to brownish . . . . WILLOW

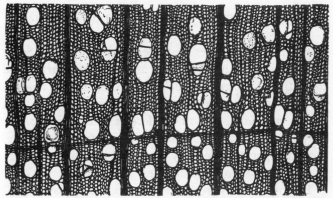

FIG. 24. Cross-section of Oregon maple (*Acer macrophyllum*), a diffuse-porous wood, showing evenly distributed pores and narrow medullary rays.

References

Bulletin 10, Forest Service, U. S. D. A., " Timber."

Bulletin 556, Forest Service, U. S. D. A., " Mechanical Properties of Woods of the United States."

Bulletin, Forest Service, U. S. D. A., " Identification of Woods Used for Ties and Timbers."

Bulletin 3, New York State College of Forestry, " Structure of Common Woods."

" American Forest Trees," Gibson, H. H. (Hardwood Record, Chicago; 1913.)

" American Woods" (sections and text), Hough, R. B. (Romeyn B. Hough, Lowville, New York.)

" Identification of the Economic Woods of the United States," Record, Samuel J. (John Wiley & Sons, Inc., New York; 1919.)

Many of the state departments of forestry, in coöperation with the United States Forest Service, have issued publications which discuss the utilization of commercial woods in those states.

PART I. THE NEEDLE–LEAF TREES

THE needle-leaf trees are of very ancient origin. Some of their remote ancestors took an important part in the formation of the great beds of coal so essential to modern civilization. At the present time this group of trees makes up a large part of the forests of the world; but they are particularly abundant in the useful forests of the north temperate zone. By " useful " is meant the value of these forests to the industries.

The trees in this group are characterized (1) by needle-like or scale-like leaves which in most cases persist for several years, (2) by dry, woody " cone " fruits which contain the seeds, (3) by the growth of branches in " whorls " about the stem, and (4) by deposits of pitch or resin in the bark or in the wood.

The needle-leaf trees of the West may be distinguished by the following key:

KEY TO THE NEEDLE-LEAF (SOFTWOOD) TREES

I. FRUIT A DRY, WOODY CONE
    A. **Leaves needle-like, long, narrow**
        1. LEAVES IN BUNDLES (EXCEPT *Pinus monophylla*)
            a. Leaves persistent, in bundles of 2 to 5   PINES (*Pinus*)
            b. Leaves deciduous, in fas-
               cicles of 15 to 25 . . . . . LARCH (*Larix*)
        2. LEAVES NOT IN BUNDLES, SINGLY ARRANGED
            a. Leaves two-ranked, opposite, twigs flat
               (1) Twigs smooth . . . . . HEMLOCK (*Tsuga*)
               (2) Twigs scaly . . . . . REDWOOD (*Sequoia*)
            b. Leaves spirally arranged, twigs irregular
               (1) Leaves flat
                   (*a*) Leaf tip sharp,
                      leaf flexible DOUGLAS FIR (*Pseudotsuga*)
                   (*b*) Leaf tip blunt, leaf brittle . . FIRS (*Abies*)
               (2) Leaves angular, four-sided . SPRUCES (*Picea*)

B. Leaves scale-like

1. LEAVES TWO-RANKED, OPPOSITE, BRANCHING FLAT
   a. *Cone round* . . . . . CEDAR (*Chamæcyparis*)
   b. *Cone oblong* . . . . . . RED CEDAR (*Thuja*)
2. LEAVES SPIRALLY ARRANGED, BRANCHING IRREGULAR
   a. *Cone round* . . . . . . CYPRESS (*Cupressus*)
   b. *Cone oblong*
      (1) Cone small, two
           fruiting scales   INCENSE CEDAR (*Libocedrus*)
      (2) Cone large, many fruiting
           scales . . . . . BIG TREE (*Sequoia*)

II. FRUIT WITH FLESHY COVERING

A. Leaves needle-like

1. SEED COMPLETELY COVERED BY
   FLESHY COVERING . . . . CALIFORNIA NUTMEG
                                      (*Tumion*)
2. SEED PARTLY COVERED BY FLESHY COV-
   ERING . . . . YEW (*Taxus*)

B. Leaves scale-like . . . . JUNIPER (*Juniperus*)

SECTION 1. TREES WITH NEEDLE–LIKE LEAVES

PINES	REDWOOD
LARCH	DOUGLAS FIR
HEMLOCK	FIRS
SPRUCES	

The Pines (*Pinus*)

From the standpoint of lumber production the pines constitute the most important group of trees in the United States. In a general way the form of the tree is ideal, the growth is rapid, and the wood product is of high technical value. Forming extensive pure stands, it makes the cost of lumbering and manufacture small. Most of the pines reproduce naturally when given protection from fire and grazing. Seedlings are easily grown in the nursery and transplanting to the field is attended with a minimum of loss. Many of the pines are of beautiful form and prove equally attractive either as ornamental trees or when grown in the woodland, shelter belt, or pasture lot.

The pines are characterized by needle-like leaves in bundles of two to five (excepting *Pinus monophylla*), by woody cones, and by a scaly bark. The group of pines having the needles in bundles of five are known as " white pines," while the others are designated " yellow pines." This distinction is based upon character of wood rather than botanical characteristics.

Twenty pines occur in the Western forest region, of which the following ten may be said to possess commercial value. The other ten pines which are not included are of limited occurrence or are of poor form and small size.

KEY TO THE PINES (*Pinus*)

A. **Needles in bundles of 5**
  1. NEEDLES SHORT, YELLOW-
      GREEN . . . . . . ROCKY MOUNTAIN WHITE PINE
                        (*P. flexilis*)
  2. NEEDLES LONG, BLUE-GREEN
    a. Bark reddish purple . . WHITE PINE (*P. monticola*)
    b. Bark reddish brown . . SUGAR PINE (*P. lambertiana*)
B. **Needles in bundles of 3**
  1. BARK RED-BROWN
    a. Cones 6 to 11 inches long . JEFFREY PINE (*P. jeffreyi*)
    b. Cones 3 to 4 inches long . YELLOW PINE (*P. ponderosa*)
  2. BARK DARK BROWN . . . . . COULTER PINE (*P. coulteri*)
C. **Needles in bundles of 2**
  1. NEEDLES LONG . . . . GRAY-LEAF PINE (*P. sabiniana*)
  2. NEEDLES SHORT
    a. Bark orange-brown . . LODGEPOLE PINE (*P. contorta*)
    b. Bark dark brown or dull brown . PIÑON PINE (*P. edulis*)
D. **Needles in bundles of 1**, singly
    arranged . . . . SINGLE-LEAF PIÑON PINE
                        (*P. monophylla*)

ROCKY MOUNTAIN WHITE PINE OR WHITE PINE *

(*Pinus flexilis*)

The Rocky Mountain white pine has a general distribution throughout the Rocky Mountains from Canada southward to the Mexican border and westward to the summit of the Sierra Nevada Mountains, occurring at elevations of 5000 to 12,000 feet. It attains its maximum development in the mountains of Arizona, where it reaches a height of 40 to 80 feet and a diameter of 2 to 5 feet.

* This species is correctly known as the Limber Pine, and this latter name should be understood wherever "Rocky Mountain white pine" appears in the section following. The earlier name is now used only in California.

Form. The stem is short, thick, rather tapering, and clear of branches for less than one fourth the total height;

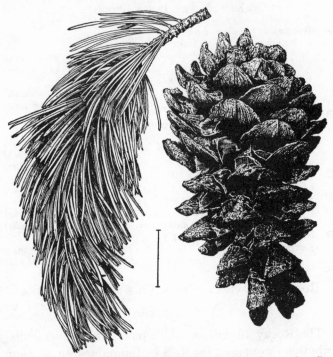

Fig. 25. Rocky Mountain white pine, showing the dense clusters of needles and the coarse, rough cone.

the crown is open, spreading, rounded, and composed of long, slender branches, which are pendulous toward the end. Young trees show distinct whorls of short, flexible, horizontal branches. The root system is deep and spreading.

Occurrence. The Rocky Mountain white pine thrives

best in the deep, moist, open soils of cañon bottoms and mountain valleys, where it occurs in mixture with white fir, sugar pine, hemlock, and lodgepole pine. It frequently occurs in exposed situations at high elevations, where the soil is thin and stony. Occasionally it forms small pure stands or groups.

Distinctive characteristics. The Rocky Mountain white pine may be distinguished by (1) the dense masses of deep yellow-green needles clustered toward the ends of the twigs; (2) the short, thick, stiff needles in bundles of 5; (3) the long (3 to 10 inches), rather cylindrical, yellow-brown cones with thickened, rounded scale tips; (4) the moderately large seeds with narrow, marginal wings; (5) the thin, smooth, light-gray bark of young stems and branches; and (6) the thick, dark-brown bark of old stems, broken into broad ridges and square plates by deep fissures.

Wood. The wood of the Rocky Mountain white pine is light, soft, moderately strong, close-grained, has a uniform texture, but is not durable; it seasons well, works easily, and takes a fine finish. The heartwood is reddish brown; the sapwood is thin and white.

Uses. Rocky Mountain white pine is used for general construction, interior finishing, flooring, shakes, farm repairs, and fuel. It is of little commercial value because of its inaccessibility, and is manufactured chiefly for local use.

The Rocky Mountain white pine is an attractive ornamental tree and is planted throughout the United States. In a clump planting it furnishes a pleasing contrast with the other white pines and spruces.

WHITE PINE *

(*Pinus monticola*)

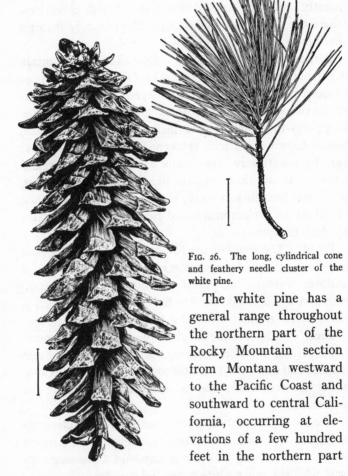

FIG. 26. The long, cylindrical cone and feathery needle cluster of the white pine.

The white pine has a general range throughout the northern part of the Rocky Mountain section from Montana westward to the Pacific Coast and southward to central California, occurring at elevations of a few hundred feet in the northern part

---

* This species is correctly known as the Western white pine, and this latter name should be understood wherever "white pine" appears in the section following.

of its range to 11,000 feet in the southern part. It reaches its best development in Idaho, where it attains a height of 100 to 150 feet and a diameter of 4 to 8 feet.

Form. The white pine closely resembles its cousin of the East in the development of one or two long branches, which give the tree an irregular, lopsided appearance. In the forest the stem is long, straight, cylindrical, and clear of branches for a considerable height; the crown is narrow and oblong.

Occurrence. White pine occurs extensively in pure stands, but is often associated with hemlock, fir, Douglas fir, and lodgepole pine in the deep, open, well-drained, sandy soils of valley bottoms, and upper slopes where the precipitation is relatively heavy.

Distinctive characteristics. White pine may be distinguished by (1) the irregular form of old trees; (2) the stout, rigid, blue-green needles in bundles of five; (3) the flexible, cylindrical cone, 5 to 11 inches long; (4) the grayish-purple, moderately thick bark (1 to $1\frac{1}{2}$ inches) with ridges broken into rectangular plates; and (5) the thin, smooth, gray bark of young stems.

Wood. The wood of the white pine is soft, light, moderately strong, close-grained, very uniform in texture, and is moderately durable; it seasons without warping and checking, is easily worked, nails without splitting, and takes paint and stain. The heartwood is cream to brownish; the sapwood is light-colored.

Uses. The white pine is classed among the important trees of the United States and is extensively used for general construction purposes. It is manufactured into lumber, lath, shingles, finishing materials, packing boxes, and crates.

The white pine is used to a considerable extent in ornamental planting throughout the northern part of the United States. The form of the young tree is pyramidal; the branches are slender and graceful. The foliage affords a pleasing contrast with any of the darker-foliaged evergreens.

SUGAR PINE

(*Pinus lambertiana*)

The sugar pine has a general distribution throughout the Pacific Coast region from Canada to Lower California, and is a characteristic tree of the Cascade, Sierra Nevada, and Coast Range mountains. It occurs at elevations of 1000 to 3000 feet in the northern part of its range to 8000 to 10,000 feet in the southern part, reaching its best development in the Cascade Mountains, where it attains a height of 200 to 250 feet and a diameter of 4 to 8 feet.

Form. The stem is long, straight, cylindrical, and clear of branches; the crown is spreading and flat, consisting of a few large branches. (See Figure 5.) It is one of the most majestic trees of the region.

Occurrence. The sugar pine is associated with yellow pine, the big tree, Douglas fir, incense cedar, and the firs in the occupation of the light soils, sandy or gravelly, of the cañon bottoms and mountain slopes. It occurs more commonly on the western slopes of the mountains where the precipitation is heavy.

Distinctive characteristics. The sugar pine may be distinguished by (1) the coarse, stiff, blue-green needles in bundles of five; (2) the flexible, cylindrical terminal cones, 12 to 24 inches long; (3) the regular whorls of

branches on the saplings and poles; (4) the deeply ridged, reddish-brown bark of old stems, broken into long, irregular plates (see Figure 8); and (5) the smooth, grayish-purple bark of young stems.

Wood. Sugar pine is soft, light, moderately strong, uniform in texture, and is moderately durable; it seasons well, is easily worked, but shows brown streaks (resin ducts) in kiln-dried stock. The heartwood is light reddish brown; the sapwood is light.

FIG. 27. The coarse, clustered needles and the long cylindrical cone of the sugar pine.

Uses. The wood is of great industrial value and is used extensively for general construction, bee supplies, pattern making, and in the manufacture of shingles, lath, interior finishing, and packing boxes.

The sugar pine is used in park and yard plantings with excellent results. The form of the young tree is pyramidal and the foliage contrasts markedly with the darker evergreens.

JEFFREY PINE

(*Pinus jeffreyi*)

The Jeffrey pine is considered by many to be a form of the yellow pine. However, the two trees differ markedly in appearance, especially when young. It is distributed over much the same territory as the yellow pine but is more common in the southern Rocky Mountains. Under favorable conditions it attains a height of 100 to 200 feet and a diameter of 3 to 7 feet. It occurs at elevations of 5000 to 9000 feet.

Form. The stem is usually rather short; the crown, composed of large and rather contorted branches, is long and irregularly oblong. Dead branches persist for many years. In the better situations the stem is long and fairly clear.

Occurrence. The Jeffrey pine occurs in extensive pure stands or in mixture with yellow pine. It is also associated with the firs and other pines but usually occupies a level belt on the mountain slope which is distinct from that of the firs above and the piñon pines below. It thrives best in the deep, moist, open, well-drained soils of the upper slopes and cañon bottoms.

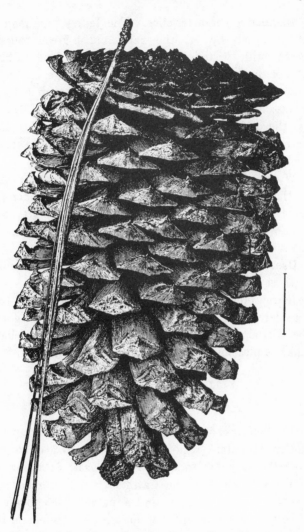

FIG. 28. Jeffrey pine. Note the three needles making up a "bundle," and the heavy, armed cone.

Distinctive characteristics. The Jeffrey pine may be distinguished by (1) the dark, bluish-green foliage; (2) the stiff, twisted needles, 4 to 9 inches long, in bundles of three (occasionally two); (3) the large, contorted branches; (4) the heavy, armed cones, from 6 to 11 inches long and 2 to 3 inches in diameter at the base; (5) the dark-brown bark of younger trees, broken into narrow ridges; and (6) the red-brown bark of old stems, broken into large, irregular plates.

Wood. The wood is as variable in texture and weight as that of the yellow pine and is marketed under the same trade names. The lumber is often knotty and inferior. The heartwood is a light yellowish brown; the sapwood is lighter in color.

Uses. The uses to which the wood is put are similar to those for yellow pine.

Jeffrey pine, as well as yellow pine, is being used to a considerable extent in ornamental plantings throughout the northern United States. The coarse, dark foliage makes a pleasing contrast with any of the white pines.

YELLOW PINE OR BULL PINE

(*Pinus ponderosa*)

The yellow or bull pine is distributed throughout the Rocky Mountain region from Canada to Mexico and from the Dakotas to the Pacific Coast, attaining its best development in the Cascades, where it reaches a height of 150 to 200 feet and a diameter of 4 to 7 feet. It occurs at elevations of from 500 to 2000 feet in the northern part of its range and from 5000 to 9000 feet in the southern part.

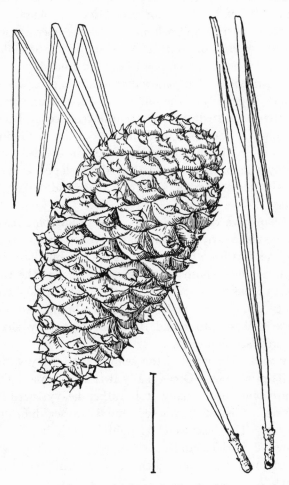

FIG. 29.   Yellow pine, showing one leaf bundle of three needles
and one of two needles.

Form. In the dense forest the stem is long, straight, and clear of branches for about half its length; the crown is narrow and columnar. In the open stands of the Black Hills of South Dakota and in the semi-desert the crown extends to a point near the ground.

Occurrence. The yellow pine occurs in extensive pure stands, especially in the southern Rocky Mountains, but is often associated with sugar pine, incense cedar, Douglas fir, big tree (Sequoia), and the firs. It is not fastidious as to its soil requirements and occurs in the deep, open, sandy soils of ridge tops and northern slopes, as well as in the moist, fertile soils of cañon and valley bottoms.

Distinctive characteristics. The yellow pine may be distinguished by (1) the dark, yellow-green, coarse, stiff needles from 5 to 11 inches long in bundles of two or three, often both on the same twig; (2) the tufted ends of naked branches; (3) the broad, oval, armed cones 3 to 6 inches long; and (4) the bright, red-brown bark broken into broad, irregular plates by shallow fissures (see Figure 7).

Wood. The wood of the yellow pine is very variable in its properties. Occasionally it is as soft and light as white pine, but usually it is rather heavy, hard, and strong; it is easily worked, but is rather difficult to season. The heartwood is light reddish brown; the sapwood is thick and pale yellow; the summer wood constitutes from one fifth to one half the annual rings.

Uses. The light, soft variety of the wood from the yellow pine is usually marketed under the trade name of " California soft pine " and is in demand for the purposes for which the sugar pine and the white pine are used. The heavier variety of the wood is used for much the same purposes as Douglas fir. In general, yellow pine is used for heavy construction, finishing materials, fencing, shingles, crossties, and fuel.

The western yellow pine has been used extensively in farm plantings throughout the northern portion of the Great Plains region, more particularly in the " sand hill " region of Nebraska, Montana, and the Dakotas. It is well suited for windbreak and shelter-belt purposes as well as for yard and roadside plantings.

COULTER PINE OR BIG-CONE PINE

(*Pinus coulteri*)

The Coulter pine has a distribution throughout the Pacific Coast region from central California to Lower California at elevations of 3000 to 6000 feet. It reaches its best development in the San Bernardino Mountains at an elevation of about 5000 feet, where it attains a height of 40 to 80 feet and a diameter of 2 to 4 feet.

Form. The stem is short, thick, straight, and clear of branches for about one fourth the total height. The crown is open, irregular, rounded, and spreading; it consists of large horizontal or slightly pendulous branches below and ascending branches above. The root system is deep and spreading.

Occurrence. The Coulter pine thrives best in the deep, more or less moist, gravelly-loam soils of the foothill slopes, where it is associated with yellow pine, in-cense cedar, and white fir. At lower elevations it is

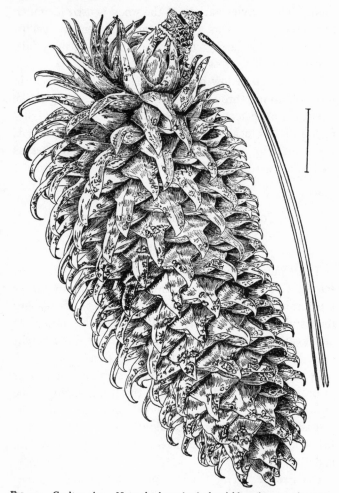

FIG. 30. Coulter pine. Note the long, hooked prickle points on the cone.

frequently associated with the chaparral. It never occurs in a pure stand.

Distinctive characteristics. The Coulter pine may be distinguished by (1) the long (6 to 12 inches), stiff, erect, bluish-green needles in bundles of three; (2) the long (9 to 14 inches), oblong, yellow-brown cones, having long, sharp, hooked prickle points on the scales, the prickle point frequently one half the length of the entire scale; (3) the large, edible seeds with wings twice as long as the seeds; (4) the rough, dark-brown to black-brown bark of old stems, broken into broad, scaly, irregularly connected ridges by deep fissures; and (5) the open, irregular crown and large persistent cones.

Wood. The wood is light, soft, brittle, coarse-grained, and not durable; it seasons well, is easily worked, and takes a fair finish. The heartwood is a pale reddish brown; the sapwood is thick and nearly white.

Uses. Coulter pine is used mostly for rough construction and fuel. It is of little commercial importance because of its poor form and inaccessibility. The seeds constitute an article of food for the native Indians.

The Coulter pine possesses some value as an ornamental tree and is occasionally planted because of the novel effect of the long needles and large cones.

Gray-leaf Pine or Digger Pine

(*Pinus sabiniana*)

The gray-leaf pine occurs commonly throughout the Pacific slope region of California at elevations of 500 to 5000 feet, reaching its best development on the western slopes of the Sierra Nevada Mountains at elevations of

FIG. 31. Gray-leaf pine, showing the leaf bundle of three needles, and the coarse, heavily armed cone.

about 2000 feet, where it attains a height of 40 to 80 feet and a diameter of 2 to 4 feet.

Form. The stem is short, more or less crooked, and splits into several large, contorted branches; the crown is open, irregular, and spreading. Young trees have a rather rounded pyramidal crown and a short, thick stem. The root system is deep and spreading.

Occurrence. The gray-leaf pine occupies the open, gravelly, or stony soils of the hot, semi-arid, interior valleys and foothills, where it forms a very open stand in the chaparral cover or mingles with yellow pine and live oak at higher elevations. In the deep, moist soils of protected situations the growth is more rapid and the form better.

Distinctive characteristics. Gray-leaf pine may be distinguished by (1) the long (8 to 12 inches), stout, grayish- or bluish-green leaves in bundles of two (or rarely three); (2) the large, heavy, persistent, grayish chestnut-brown, heavily armed cones, from 6 to 10 inches long and 4 to 6 inches thick; (3) the large, edible seeds with wings half the length of the seed; (4) the smooth, dull-gray bark of young stems and branches; (5) the thick, dark grayish-brown bark of old stems, broken into broad, scaly, irregularly connected ridges by deep fissures; and (6) the sparse foliage and open, irregular form.

Wood. The wood is light, soft, brittle, even-textured, cross-grained, and not durable; it seasons well, works easily, and takes a fine finish. The heartwood is a dark yellow-brown; the sapwood is thick and nearly white.

Uses. Gray-leaf pine is utilized chiefly for fuel within its range. It is of no commercial importance because of the poor form and very open stand. A medicinal oil is distilled from the resinous juices. The seeds constitute an important article of food for the native Indians.

In the better situations the gray-leaf pine makes a rapid growth and under such conditions it is an ornamental tree of some local importance. The large, persistent cones and gray-green foliage make an attractive appearance.

LODGEPOLE PINE

(*Pinus contorta*)

The lodgepole pine is distributed throughout the Rocky Mountain system from Canada to Mexico, occurring at elevations of sea level to 5000 feet in the northern part of its range and 7000 to 11,500 feet in the southern part. It reaches its best development in the high, bench-like plateaus, where it attains a height of from 70 to 150 feet and a diameter of 2 to 6 feet. Two forms are recognized — the sand-dune tree of the coast and the mountain tree.

Form. In the open the stem is short and the crown long and pyramidal. The forest-grown tree produces a long, straight, cylindrical, clear stem and a small, narrow, spire-like crown of small branches. The root system is spreading.

Occurrence. In the high mountains the lodgepole pine occurs in dense, pure, even-aged stands; on the coast it is found in open, pure stands. Frequently it occurs in mixture with the firs, white pine, and Douglas

fir about the margins of mountain meadows. However, it thrives best in the deep, moist, well-drained,
open soils of the high mountain benches.

FIG. 32.   Lodgepole pine.   Cluster of coarse needles and small, armed cones
at the end of a branch.

Distinctive characteristics.   The lodgepole pine may
be distinguished by (1) the pyramidal or spire-like form;
(2) the short, yellow-green needles in bundles of two;
(3) the small, armed cone, which persists for years;
(4) the thin ($\frac{1}{4}$ inch), light, orange-brown bark covered

with thin, loose scales; and (5) the dense, even-aged stands.

Wood. The wood is soft, light, weak, straight-grained, often shows a "dimpled" effect, is of uniform texture, and not durable; it seasons well and is easily worked. The heartwood is a pale yellow; the sapwood is similar.

Uses. Lodgepole pine is much in demand for derrick and rickerpole purposes by the mountain farmers. It is used also for rough construction, fencing, mine timbers, and fuel.

It has a very distinctive form and coloring and is occasionally used in ornamental planting. It also possesses considerable value for watershed planting at high elevations.

The Piñon Pines

The piñon pines, of which there are four, are distributed throughout the southwestern United States, extending northward to Wyoming and westward into California. They occur in moderately high altitudes, bounded by the yellow and Jeffrey pines above and by the yucca and sagebrush below. While they often form extensive pure stands, they are more often associated with the desert junipers, mountain mahogany, and Jeffrey pine. They possess considerable value for purposes of watershed protection and in the prevention of wind erosion.

The different species may be distinguished by the leaves, as follows:

1. Leaves short, stout, in bundles of four . . . FOUR-LEAF PINE
   (*P. quadrifolia*)
2. Leaves short, slender, in bundles of three . . MEXICAN PIÑON
   (*P. cembroides*)

3. Leaves short, stout, in bundles of two　Piñon pine (*P. edulis*)
4. Leaves short, stout, round, single . . . . Single-leaf pine
(*P. monophylla*)

Space can be given here only to a description of the more important piñon pines — the single-leaf pine and the piñon pine.

Piñon Pine or Nut Pine

(*Pinus edulis*)

The piñon pine occurs commonly at elevations of 4000 to 8000 feet throughout the desert ranges of the southwestern United States from Texas to Arizona and from Wyoming to the Mexican border. It reaches its best development in New Mexico, where it attains a height of 30 to 40 feet and a diameter of 1 to 3 feet (ground level).

Form. The stem is short, thick, tapering, and clear of branches for but a few feet above ground level; the crown is open and irregular, and consists of a few large,

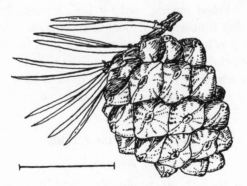

Fig. 33. Piñon pine, showing the needles in groups of
two, and the small oval cone.

contorted branches.   The root system is deep and spreading.

Occurrence.   The piñon pine thrives in the deep, open soils of the desert foothills in which the level of ground water is at a depth of 20 or more feet.   It occurs in extensive, open, pure stands or in mixture with the desert junipers, Jeffrey pine, and mountain mahogany.

Distinctive characteristics.   The piñon pine may be distinguished by (1) the short (about 1 inch), stiff, more or less twisted, dark-green needles in bundles of two (or rarely three); (2) the short, oblong, orange-brown cones with thickened, rounded scale tips. and large edible seeds; (3) the thin ($\frac{1}{2}$ to $\frac{3}{4}$ inch), scaly, light-brown bark of old stems, broken into irregularly connected ridges by shallow fissures; and (4) the irregular form.

Wood.   The wood is light, soft, dense, brittle, has even texture, and is not durable; it seasons well, works easily, and takes a fair finish.   The heartwood is creamy brown; the sapwood is thin and nearly white.

Uses.   Piñon pine is used for fuel, fencing, farm repairs, mine timbers, and rough construction.   In some sections it is burned for charcoal to be used in smelting. It is the principal fuel-wood tree of the region.

The seeds are collected by the Indians as an article of food; large quantities are also shipped to the cities to be used in confections.

SINGLE-LEAF PIÑON PINE

(*Pinus monophylla*)

The single-leaf piñon pine is found in semi-desert situations at elevations of 2000 to 8000 feet, from Utah westward to California and southward into Arizona. The tree does not often exceed a height of 25 or 30 feet and a diameter of 12 to 15 inches.

Fig. 34. Single-leaf pine. Above is an end twig, showing the cylindrical, pointed needles; below is an open cone; in the center is a cone scale with seed attached and a single seed removed from the scale.

Form. The stem is short, frequently dividing a few feet above ground; the crown is open and spreading, consisting of a few large, irregular branches. The tree has a taproot system, which penetrates deeply into the earth.

Occurrence. The single-leaf piñon pine is primarily a tree of the semi-arid regions, clothing the upper slopes of the desert ranges. It occurs commonly in coarse, gravelly soils and shallow deposits, where it is associated with junipers and chaparral.

Distinctive characteristics. The single-leaf piñon pine may be distinguished by (1) the short stem and contorted branches; (2) the open crown and silvery-green foliage; and (3) the large seeds in rather small yellowish-green cones.

Wood. The wood is light, soft, brittle, close-grained, and uniform in texture; it seasons well and works easily. The heartwood is yellowish; the sapwood is lighter in color.

Uses. The seed is edible and over much of the tree's range it constitutes an important article of food. The wood is used for fuel, fencing, charcoal, and occasionally for saw lumber. Because of the limited tree growth of the region, the single-leaf piñon pine is given a value greatly in excess of that accorded a tree of similar form in a timbered region.

Larch, Red Fir, or Tamarack

(*Larix occidentalis*)

The larch, often erroneously called "red fir" by lumbermen, is confined to elevations of 2000 to 7000

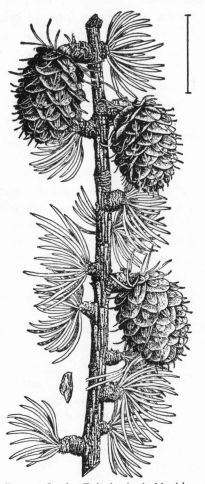

FIG. 35. Larch. Twig showing leaf fascicles, leaf knobs, and cones. Note the winged seed shown beside the twig.

feet and is distributed throughout the northern Rocky Mountain system, extending southward into Montana, Idaho, Washington, and Oregon. It reaches its best development in western Montana, where it attains a height of 200 to 250 feet and a diameter of 4 to 8 feet.

Form. The stem is long, straight, cylindrical, and clear of branches; the crown is open, flat, and pyramidal. From the standpoint of wood production, it approaches closely to the ideal. The root system is spreading.

Occurrence. Occasionally the larch occurs in pure stands but usually it is found in mixture with Douglas fir, the firs, the spruces, white pine, and lodgepole pine. While it thrives best in a deep, moist, open, well-drained soil, it usually occupies the moist northern slopes, high benches, and the stream and valley bottoms.

Distinctive characteristics. The larch may be distinguished by (1) the short (1 to 2 inches), rigid, sharp, pale-green needles in clusters of twenty to thirty; (2) the small (1 to $1\frac{1}{2}$ inches) reflex cone, with papery scales; (3) the thick, red-brown bark broken into irregular oblong plates 2 to 3 inches long; and (4) the shedding of the leaves in the autumn.

Wood. The wood is rather heavy, hard, strong, rather coarse-grained, compact, satiny, resinous, and durable; it seasons badly, is rather difficult to work, but takes a fine polish. The heartwood is a bright reddish brown; the sapwood is thin and white. The wood resembles that of the Douglas fir.

Uses. Larch is in demand for ship timbers and for heavy construction. It is manufactured into finishing materials, cabinet stock, flooring, and interior finishing.

Locally it is used for fencing, telegraph and telephone poles, crossties, and mine timbers.

The larch does not thrive outside of its natural range and for this reason is of little value for ornamental purposes.

Hemlock

(*Tsuga heterophylla*)

The hemlock is distributed throughout the northern part of the Rocky Mountain system from Canada to central California and from Montana to the Coast. It is found at varying elevations, from sea level to 7000 feet. It reaches its best development in the coastal region of Oregon and Washington, where it attains a height of 125 to 200 feet and a diameter of 5 to 10 feet.

Form. The crown is pyramidal, narrow, and deep, and is composed of small branches which are quite persistent; the stem is straight, cylindrical, and clear for about half its length. In the open it retains its branches near the ground until it enters the standard stage. The root system is spreading.

Occurrence. The hemlock thrives best in the deep, moist, open soils of the river bottoms, flats, and lower slopes of the mountains, where it is associated with Douglas fir, sugar pine, incense cedar, and lowland fir.

Distinctive characteristics. Hemlock may be distinguished by (1) the short ($\frac{1}{4}$ to 1 inch), two-ranked, flat, soft, lustrous, dark-green, solitary needles; (2) the small cones (1 inch), which have soft, papery scales; (3) the thin, finely scaled brown bark of young stems; and (4) the moderately thick (1 to $1\frac{1}{2}$ inches), hard, deeply furrowed bark of old trees, the wide, flat ridges of which are connected by narrow cross ridges.

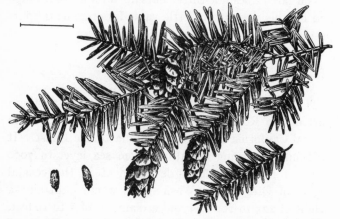

Fig. 36. The small, soft cone and the short, blunt needles of hemlock. Two seeds are shown in the lower left-hand corner.

Wood. The wood is moderately heavy, strong, stiff, tough, hard, fairly uniform in texture, has a rather attractive grain, and is moderately durable; it seasons well, works fairly easily, and takes a fine polish. The heartwood is a pale reddish brown; the sapwood is thin and nearly white.

Uses. Hemlock is used for slack cooperage, fruit barrels, cheap furniture, burial boxes, interior finishing, office fixtures, flooring, and paper pulp. A large percentage of the cut is used in the manufacture of packing boxes and crates. The bark is rich in tannic acid and is in demand by the tanneries.

Seedling and sapling hemlocks possess a very attractive form and are used to a considerable extent in ornamental planting. With a little care, this tree thrives in any deep, moist, well-drained soil.

Redwood

(*Sequoia sempervirens*)

The redwood has a rather restricted range, from southern Oregon to southern California, forming a narrow belt ten to thirty miles wide along the coast. It occurs from sea level to elevations of 2500 feet in the Coast Range, where it attains a height of 200 to 350 feet and a diameter of 8 to 20 feet.

Form. The tree is greatly buttressed at its base and produces a tall, cylindrical, straight stem, which is clear of branches for one third to one half the total height. The crown of younger trees extends almost to the ground and is composed of small branches, narrowly pyramidal. Older trees develop a rounded, flat, spreading crown of large branches at right angles to the stem.

Occurrence. The redwood occupies the moist situations of the western slopes of the mountains — more especially the lower slopes — the protected flats and valley bottoms, and the river deltas. It occurs in extensive pure stands and also in mixture with hemlock, spruce, fir, cedar, and the hardwoods. It thrives best in the region of heavy sea fogs.

Distinctive characteristics. The redwood may be distinguished by (1) the sharp-pointed, flat, short ($\frac{1}{2}$ inch), needle-shaped (rather scale-like on the older twigs), glossy, deep yellow-green leaves; (2) the persistent dead leaves which stay on the tree for a year or two; (3) the small ($\frac{1}{2}$ to 1 inch), globular, terminal cones with shield-shaped scales, each covering four or

FIG. 37. Redwood. Twig showing the flat needles and small terminal cones. Note the scale-like leaves at the tips of the branches.

five flat, winged seeds; and (4) the thick (8 to 12 inches), fibrous, soft, cinnamon-brown bark of old stems, broken into long, broad ridges by deep fissures (see Figure 11).

Wood. The wood is soft, light, brittle, weak, splits easily, has a coarse texture, a distinct grain, but is very durable; it is easily worked and takes polish well. The heartwood is a dark red-brown, with a purplish tinge; the sapwood is thin and white.

Uses. Redwood is used for general construction, shingles, sawed poles and posts, grape supports, foundation blocks, siding, interior finishing, door panels, sashes and doors, office fixtures, etc. It is particularly valuable for the production of large-sized dimension stock.

The redwood is one of the most beautiful and graceful ornamental trees and is extensively used on the Pacific coast and in the southern United States. Seedlings are easily produced and stand transplanting very well. It is not affected by temperatures as low as 0° F.

Douglas Fir, Douglas Spruce, Red Fir, or Oregon Pine
(*Pseudotsuga taxifolia*)

The Douglas fir, or red fir as it is often called, is not a true fir, although it somewhat resembles a fir. It is distributed over the entire Rocky Mountain system from Canada southward to Mexico and from Colorado and Arizona westward to the Coast, occurring from sea level to elevations of 10,000 feet. It reaches its best development on the western slopes of the Cascade Range, where it attains a height of 150 to 200 feet and a diameter of 4 to 10 feet. A flagpole made from a Douglas fir (at Kew Gardens, England) is 160 feet long, and measures 36 inches at the butt and 6 inches at the top.

Form. The stem is long, straight, cylindrical, and clear of branches for one half to three fourths the total height; the lower branches are horizontal or slightly drooping and the upper branches are ascending, giving the crown a pyramidal form which is broad at the base and sharply pointed. Old specimens develop a small, flat, rounded crown of large branches.   The root system is deep and spreading.

Fɪɢ. 38.   Branch of Douglas fir, showing the feathered appendages on the cone scales, and the winged seed.

Occurrence.   The Douglas fir thrives best in the deep, moist, open, sandy, well-drained soils of northern slopes and benches and the sheltered cañons of the higher mountains.   It is associated with the yellow pine, the sugar pine, hemlock, incense cedar, redwood, and fir, but it frequently occurs in extensive, nearly pure stands.

Distinctive characteristics.   The Douglas fir may be distinguished by (1) the sharp-pointed, flat, short ($\frac{3}{4}$ to

1 inch), solitary, lustrous, yellow-green or blue-green leaves; (2) the small (2 to 3 inches), feathered, red-brown cones; (3) the thin, ashy-brown, chalky, patched bark of young stems; and (4) the thick (5 to 20 inches), rough, dark-brown bark of old trees, which is characterized by broad ridges divided by deep fissures.

Wood. The wood is heavy, hard, strong, stiff, rather fine-grained, and durable; it seasons well, works fairly easily, and when finished has a pronounced and very attractive grain. The wood in general compares favorably with the yellow pine (*Pinus palustris*) of the South. The heartwood is orange to reddish; the sapwood is thin and white. Lumbermen recognize two types — the "red" and the "yellow," based on the color of the heartwood.

Uses. Douglas fir is used for heavy construction, boat timbers, railway-car construction, agricultural implements and vehicles, office fixtures, furniture, refrigerators, musical instruments, finishing materials, veneer, mine timbers, fencing, and crossties.

Because of its hardiness, graceful form, and attractive foliage, the Douglas fir is extensively used in the United States and Europe for ornamental purposes.

The Firs (*Abies*)

The true firs occur commonly throughout the Western forest region but at relatively high elevations, frequently forming extensive pure stands. The form is less desirable than that of the pines, as the stem tapers rather noticeably and the branches persist on the lower stem. The wood, too, is rather inferior and usually shows characteristic defects.

The cones stand erect on slender branchlets, the central core persisting after the scales have fallen away. The leaves are arranged singly on the twig in spiral form and are soft to the touch and brittle in texture. When the leaves are stripped, the twig is smooth. The bark shows characteristic " blisters " filled with resin.

The firs are beautiful ornamental trees; the form is conical and rather spire-tipped, the branching dense, and the color distinctive.

KEY TO THE FIRS

A. Bark red-brown
    1. CONES NOT FEATHERED . . . . RED FIR (*A. magnifica*)
    2. CONES FEATHERED . . . . . NOBLE FIR (*A. nobilis*)
B. Bark ashy gray
    1. CONES PURPLE . . . . . . ALPINE FIR (*A. lasiocarpa*)
    2. CONES YELLOW-GREEN
        a. Needles blue-green . . . . WHITE FIR (*A. concolor*)
        b. Needles yellow-green . . . LOWLAND FIR (*A. grandis*)

RED FIR

(*Abies magnifica*)

The red fir is found, at elevations of 5000 to 10,000 feet, from southern Oregon to Lower California. It reaches its best development in eastern Oregon, where it attains a height of from 125 to 250 feet and a diameter of 2 to 10 feet.

Form. In the open the tree develops a short, tapering stem and a long, dense, narrowly conical crown with a rounded top. In the dense forest the stem is straight, cylindrical, and free from branches for about half its total height. The lower branches droop noticeably.

Occurrence. The red fir is associated with Douglas fir, incense cedar, and white fir in the moist situations of the Coast ranges and Cascades.   It thrives best in

FIG. 39.   Portion of a branch and the large, erect cone of the red fir.

the open, moist, sandy soils of sheltered meadows, cañons, and benches of the western slopes.

Distinctive characteristics. The red fir may be distinguished by (1) the short (1 inch), stiff, flat blue-green needles, crowded toward the upper side of the twig; (2) the large (6 to 8 inches), cylindrical, erect, smooth, dark-purple cones; (3) the hard, rough, moderately thick (2 to 3 inches), red-brown bark broken into narrow, rounded ridges by deep fissures.

Wood. The wood is light, soft, weak, close-grained, of fine texture, and is moderately durable; it seasons fairly well, is easily worked, but is apt to check when dried too rapidly. The heartwood is red or reddish brown; the sapwood is white.

Uses. Red fir is used for general construction and in the manufacture of packing boxes and crates, flooring, interior finishing, sashes and doors, etc. It is also an important source of fuel wood.

The red fir is unsurpassed for beauty and symmetry by any of the conifers and is a favorite with landscape gardeners for park planting. It thrives on any deep, moist, well-drained soil and young stock is easily handled. It is perhaps one of the most distinctive trees of the region.

NOBLE FIR, RED FIR, OR LARCH

(*Abies nobilis*)

The noble fir, often erroneously called " larch " by lumbermen, occurs at elevations of 2000 to 6000 feet in the Cascade and Coast ranges of the Pacific Coast states, from Canada to central California. It reaches its best

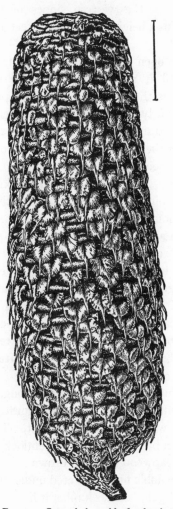
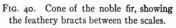

FIG. 40.   Cone of the noble fir, showing
the feathery bracts between the scales.

development on the western slopes of the Cascades, where it attains a height of 100 to 225 feet and a diameter of 2 to 8 feet.

Form. In open stands the tree retains its lower branches until it reaches the standard stage; under such conditions the stem is short and tapering and the crown is narrowly pyramidal. In the dense forest the stem is long, straight, cylindrical, and clear of branches for about half the total height, and the crown is broadly conical. The root system is deep and spreading.

Occurrence. Associated with hemlock, Douglas fir, and lodgepole pine, the noble fir occupies the moist situations throughout its range. However, it thrives under cultivation in any deep, open, moist, well-drained soil.

Distinctive characteristics. The noble fir may be distinguished by (1) the short (1 to 1½ inches), sharp, flat, silvery blue-green needles, apparently clustered on the upper side of the twig; (2) the large (4 to 6 inches), cylindrical, feathered, yellow-green, erect cones; (3) the moderately thick (1 to 2 inches), bright red-brown bark broken into broad ridges by deep longitudinal fissures and shallow cross fissures.

Wood. The wood is light, hard, strong, rather close-grained, of uniform texture, but not durable; it seasons well, is easily worked, and holds paint. The heartwood is light reddish brown, resembling hemlock (*Tsuga heterophylla*); the sapwood is a dull brown.

Uses. The noble fir is marketed under the trade name of "Western larch," and as lumber it has been introduced all over the United States. It is used for general construction, interior finishing, car.construction, door panels, sash and door construction, and packing boxes and crates. Of all the firs of the United States, its wood is considered to be of the highest commercial value.

The noble fir is used extensively in Europe for ornamental purposes and is considered to be one of the best of the introduced trees. It has been planted in the United States to a small extent very successfully. Its use should be greatly extended.

ALPINE FIR OR BALSAM FIR
(*Abies lasiocarpa*)

The alpine fir has a general distribution throughout the Rocky Mountains from Canada southward to a point near the Mexican border, occurring at elevations of 2000 to 3000 feet in the northern part of its range, and at elevations of 8000 to 12,000 feet in the southern part. It reaches its best development in Washington and Idaho, where it attains a height of 80 to 160 feet and a diameter of 2 to 5 feet.

Form. The stem is short, tapering, and clear of branches for less than one fourth the total height; the crown is dense, conical, and terminates in a spire-like point. The lower branches are rather pendulous; the upper branches are ascending. The root system is spreading.

Occurrence. The alpine fir thrives best in the deep, moist, open soils of protected mountain valleys at high elevations. Frequently it forms extensive pure stands on the upper slopes at or near the timber line. Ordinarily it is associated with Engelmann spruce, hemlock, white pine, and yellow cedar.

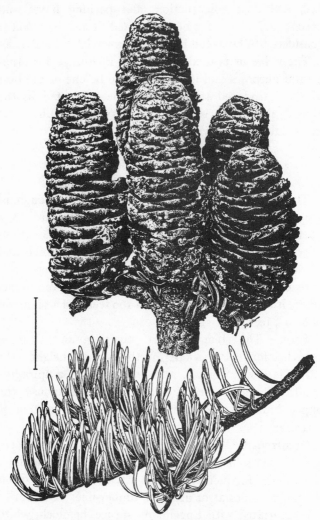

FIG. 41. Cluster of cones and portion of branch of the alpine fir.

Distinctive characteristics. The alpine fir may be distinguished by (1) the long (1 inch), flat, blunt, blue-green needles, crowded toward the upper side of the twig; (2) the cylindrical, deep-purple, velvety, thin-scaled cones, from 2 to 4 inches long; (3) the resin-covered buds; (4) the grayish twigs, which are slightly hairy; (5) the thin, hard, flinty, ashy-gray bark of old stems, unbroken except for the irregular, shallow fissures dividing broad, flat ridges near the base; (6) the spire-like tip of the crown; and (7) the pendulous lower branches, which persist to a point near the ground.

Wood. The wood is soft, light, brittle, fine-grained, of uniform texture, rather knotty, and not durable; it seasons well, works easily, and takes a fair finish. The heartwood is a pale yellow-brown; the sapwood is pale yellow. It has a distinctive, mildly rank odor.

Uses. Alpine fir is used for fuel, mine timbers, and rough construction. It is of little commercial value because of its poor form and inaccessibility. When it occurs in mixture with associated trees, it is usually manufactured with them.

The alpine fir is an attractive ornamental tree and is used to a limited extent over the entire northern United States and in Europe. The dense, pyramidal form of young trees and the blue-green foliage are very attractive.

WHITE FIR

(*Abies concolor*)

The white fir is distributed throughout the Rocky Mountain system from Canada southward to Mexico and from Colorado westward to California, occurring at elevations of 2000 to 11,000 feet. It reaches its best

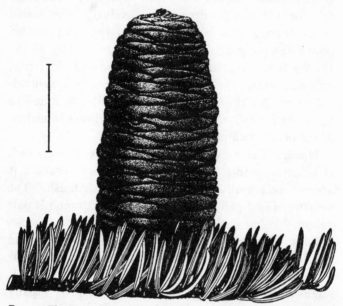

FIG. 42. The erect, cylindrical cone and closely arranged needles of the white fir.

development on the Pacific slope, where it attains a height of 150 to 250 feet and a diameter of 3 to 6 feet.

Form. In the open the stem is short; the crown is dense and has a rounded pyramidal form, with branches extending to a point near the ground. (See Figure 4.) In the forest the stem is straight, tapering, and clear for about half the total height. Young trees have a dense crown, are pyramidal in form, and very regular in outline.

Occurrence.   The white fir thrives best in the deep, open, moist, well-drained soils of northern slopes, benches, and cañon bottoms, where it is associated with Douglas fir, white spruce, aspen, and occasionally with yellow pine.   It often occurs in small, pure groups.

Distinctive characteristics.   White fir may be distinguished by (1) the flat, long (1 to 2 inches), blunt, solitary, light bluish-green needles which strip from the surface, leaving the twig smooth; (2) the erect, cylindrical, yellowish-green cones, 3 to 5 inches long; (3) the smooth grayish bark of young stems and branches; and (4) the thick (4 to 6 inches), hard, horny, ashy-gray bark of old stems, broken into broad ridges by deep fissures.

Wood.   The wood is light, soft, weak, brittle, rather coarse-grained, and not durable; it seasons well, works easily, and takes paint satisfactorily.   The heartwood is light brown; the sapwood is yellowish.   " Wind shake " is a natural defect which is very common in white fir, especially in the larger trees.

Uses.   White fir is used for structural timbers, rough construction, packing boxes and crates, butter tubs, and wooden ware.   Locally it is used for mine timbers, fencing, and general construction.

Because of its hardiness, symmetrical form, and attractive appearance, the white fir has been extensively planted for ornamental purposes both in the United States and in Europe.   Many horticultural varieties based on the leaf color and the form of the tree have been developed.

LOWLAND FIR

(*Abies grandis*)

The range of the lowland fir covers the northern part of the Rocky Mountain system from Canada southward to central California and from Montana westward to the Coast. Within its range it occurs at various elevations, from sea level to 7000 feet. It reaches its best development in the bottom lands near the Coast, where it attains a height of 200 to 300 feet and a diameter of 3 to 6 feet.

Form. In open stand the stem is short, and the crown is spire-tipped and narrowly conical, the lower branches drooping noticeably. In the dense forest the stem is long, straight, cylindrical, and clear of branches for about half the total height. The root system is spreading.

Occurrence. The lowland fir occupies moist situations in cañon bottoms, high benches, and northern slopes, although it thrives best in a deep, moist, well-drained soil. It seldom occurs as a pure stand but is usually associated with Douglas fir, red cedar, cottonwood, white pine, larch, and spruce.

Distinctive characteristics. Lowland fir may be distinguished by (1) the short (1 to 2 inches), blunt, flat, solitary, shiny, yellow-green needles, which are so twisted that they appear two-ranked on the twig; (2) the short (2 to 4 inches), erect, conical, yellow-green cones; (3) the thin, smooth, ashy-brown, chalky, blotched bark of young stems; and (4) the moderately thick (1 to 2 inches), hard, horny, ashy-gray bark of old trees, broken into long, sharp ridges by shallow, narrow fissures.

Wood. The wood is light, soft, weak, brittle, has a rather coarse but straight grain, and is not durable;

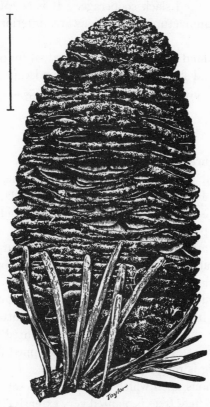

Fig. 43. Cone and cluster of needles of the lowland fir.

it seasons well, works easily, and takes paint satisfactorily. The heartwood is a pale yellowish or reddish brown; the sapwood is yellowish.

Uses. The wood is marketed under the trade name of "fir" and is used for rough construction, packing boxes and crates, and slack cooperage. It is adapted for use in the manufacture of woodenware, interior finishing, etc.

The lowland fir is used to a small extent for ornamental planting and should find favor with landscape gardeners. In the youthful stages the form and foliage are both very attractive.

The Spruces (*Picea*)

The spruces occur very generally in the Western forest region, but always at higher elevations where the precipitation is heavy and the temperature relatively low. The form is rather poor; the stem tapers rapidly and the branches persist on the lower stem. The wood is of high commercial value, and for many purposes, the equal of pine. Usually they occur in dense pure stands but at rather inaccessible altitudes.

The spruces are characterized by pendent cones, which fall soon after the seed is scattered in the autumn. The leaves are singly arranged but sharp-pointed and harsh to the touch. When the leaves are stripped the surface of the twig is rough to the touch because of the minute bark cushions upon which the needles are set.

This group of trees is planted very extensively throughout the United States and Europe for ornamental purposes. The form is broadly pyramidal; the crown is dense and the branches persist to a point near the ground. Many horticultural varieties possess distinctive and attractive coloring.

Key to the Spruces

A. **Leaves yellow-green** . . . . Sitka spruce (*P. sitchensis*)
B. **Leaves blue-green**
   1. Bark brownish purple   White spruce (*P. engelmanni*)
   2. Bark dark grayish brown   Blue spruce (*P. parryana*)

Sitka Spruce or Tideland Spruce

(*Picea sitchensis*)

The Sitka, or tideland, spruce is distributed through the Cascade and Coast ranges from Canada to central California, occurring at elevations of 2000 to 4000 feet. It reaches its best development in Washington and Oregon, where it attains a height of 80 to 150 feet and a diameter of from 3 to 6 feet. Occasional specimens reach a height of 200 feet and a diameter of 15 feet.

Form. In general, the tree develops a long, tapering, moderately clear stem and an open, broadly pyramidal crown of large branches. The stem is buttressed. The root system is deep and spreading.

Occurrence. The Sitka spruce occupies the moist northern and western slopes of the mountains, where the precipitation is heavy and where the sea fogs are characteristic. Usually it is associated with the white pine, sugar pine, lodgepole pine, Douglas fir, and hemlock.

Distinctive characteristics. Sitka spruce may be distinguished by (1) the solitary, sharp, flat (indistinctly four-sided), bright yellow-green needles; (2) the small, soft, cylindrical, purplish terminal cones, from 2 to 4 inches long; (3) the thin ($\frac{1}{2}$ inch), purplish- or reddish-brown bark, which has large, easily detached scales.

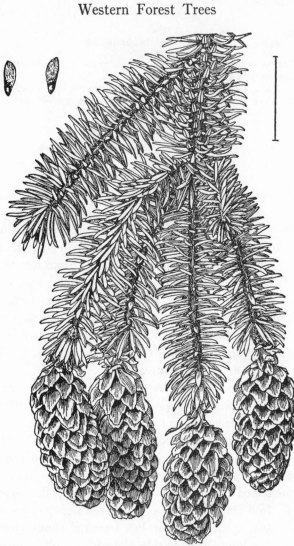

FIG. 44. Branch of Sitka spruce, showing a cluster of the pendulous terminal cones. Note the two seeds in the upper left-hand corner.

Wood. The wood is light, soft, medium strong, of uniform texture, but not durable; it seasons well, is easily worked, and takes a finish well. The heartwood is pale brown; the sapwood is lighter in color.

Uses. Sitka spruce is used for general construction purposes, finishing materials, musical instruments, boat construction, vehicles, agricultural implements, woodenware, packing boxes and crates, pulp wood, etc. While not so strong as Douglas fir, the wood ranks second to it in commercial importance.

Sitka spruce presents an attractive appearance and is used to a limited extent for ornamental purposes. As with most of the spruces, it transplants easily and grows with fair rapidity.

WHITE SPRUCE OR ENGELMANN SPRUCE *

(*Picea engelmanni*)

The white spruce occurs commonly throughout the Rocky Mountain system from Canada southward to Mexico and from Montana and Colorado westward to the Coast. It attains its best development in the northern part of its range, where it reaches a height of 100 to 150 feet and a diameter of 3 to 5 feet. It is found at elevations of 5000 to 12,000 feet.

Form. The forest-grown white spruce develops a long, straight, clear stem and a dense, narrow, pyramidal crown of small branches. In the open the tree retains its branches to a point near the ground. The root system is deep and spreading.

Occurrence. The white spruce thrives best in deep, moist, open soils, and in the cooler situations of northern

* The white spruce and Engelmann spruce are now recognized as two distinct species. The section following actually refers to the Engelmann spruce, and this latter name should be understood wherever "white spruce" appears.

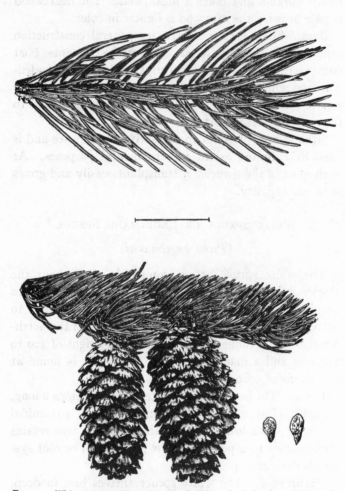

Fig. 45. White spruce. Above is a "leader" branch; below is a side branch and open cones. Two seeds are shown in lower right-hand corner.

slopes and benches where the growing season is short
and the precipitation is heavy and mostly in the form of
snow. It occurs in extensive pure stands and also in
mixture with Douglas fir, hemlock, lodgepole pine, and
the firs.

Distinctive characteristics. The white spruce may be
distinguished by (1) the four-angled, short (1 inch),
soft needles, set singly on the twig and curving upwards
on lateral branches; (2) the deep blue-green, dense
foliage; (3) the hanging, soft-scaled cones, 2 to 3 inches
long; (4) the thin, dark brownish-purple bark which has
small, loosely attached scales. The bruised twigs emit
a disagreeable odor.

Wood. The wood is light, weak, soft, close-grained,
dents without splitting, and is not durable; it seasons
well and is easily worked. The heartwood is a pale yellow, tinged with red; the sapwood is white. The lumber
shows many small knots.

Uses. The white spruce is used for general construction purposes, for posts, poles, and fuel. It is also
manufactured into finishing materials, boat stock, and
charcoal. The bark furnishes tannic acid.

White spruce is used to a limited extent for ornamental
purposes; the youthful form and the dark silvery blue-
green foliage make a very attractive effect.

BLUE SPRUCE OR COLORADO BLUE SPRUCE

(*Picea parryana*)

The blue spruce has a general distribution throughout
the northern part of the Rocky Mountain system from
Canada southward to central California and Colorado,

reaching its best development in Colorado and Wyoming, where it attains a height of 100 to 150 feet and a diameter of 2 to 4 feet. It is found at elevations of 1000 to 10,000 feet.

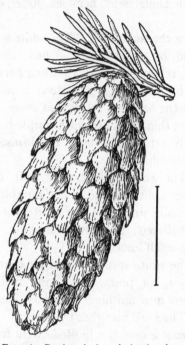

FIG. 46. Portion of a branch showing the sharp, stiff needles and pendulous cone of the blue spruce.

Form. In its youth the crown is densely pyramidal, the branches persisting to the ground. In the forest the stem is never clear for more than half the total height and the crown is narrowly pyramidal. The root system is deep and spreading.

Occurrence. The blue spruce occupies the moist northern slopes and the benches at high elevations where the precipitation is heavy. It is associated with white spruce, hemlock, and the firs.

Distinctive characteristics. The blue spruce may be distinguished by (1) the solitary, stiff, sharp, four-sided needles about an inch long; (2) the light-brown, hanging, rough, cylindrical cones, 3 to 5 inches long; and (3) the thin, dark grayish-brown bark, covered with loose scales. One variety possesses bright silvery blue-green foliage.

Wood. The wood is light, soft, weak, uniform in texture, and not durable; it seasons well and is easily worked. The heartwood is nearly white; the sapwood is similar in color.

Uses. Blue spruce is used locally for fuel, mine timbers, fencing, and general construction. It is marketed with white spruce and is used for similar purposes.

The " blue " variety is one of the most attractive and most highly cherished of the ornamental trees. It is equally satisfactory either as an isolated specimen or as part of a group planting. The blue spruce is not fastidious as to soil requirements and thrives throughout the northern United States and Europe.

SECTION 2. TREES WITH SCALE–LIKE LEAVES

TRUE CEDARS	BIG TREE
RED CEDAR	CALIFORNIA NUTMEG
MONTEREY CYPRESS	YEW
INCENSE CEDAR	JUNIPERS

The Cedars (*Chamæcyparis*)

The true cedars constitute a rather small group of trees, but they grow to a large size and are of high commercial importance. The wood is soft, light, very durable, and is characterized by a pronounced odor. It is frequently substituted for white pine and spruce in the arts.

In all the cedars the bark is ridged and stringy, the leaves are scale-like, and the cone is round and composed of shield-shaped scales.

Several other trees called " cedar " do not belong to this group; as, for example, the red cedar and the incense cedar. These two species belong to two separate and distinct groups or genera.

KEY TO THE CEDARS

A. Bark ashy gray; leaves sharp, harsh . . . . YELLOW CEDAR
(*C. nootkatensis*)
B. Bark cinnamon-brown; leaves soft . . . PORT ORFORD CEDAR
(*C. lawsoniana*)

YELLOW CEDAR, YELLOW CYPRESS, OR SITKA CYPRESS

(*Chamæcyparis nootkatensis*)

The yellow cedar is confined to the coast ranges of Washington and Oregon, occurring from sea level to

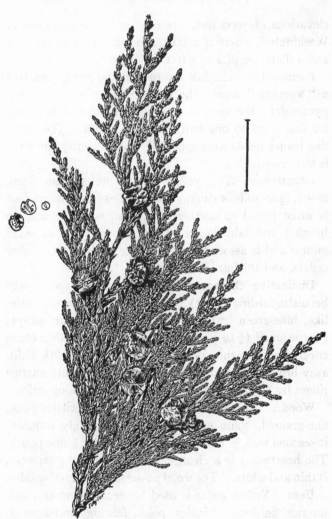

FIG. 47. Branch of yellow cedar, showing the globose cones. At the side is a group of seeds; the one at the right is shown natural size, the others are twice natural size.

elevations of 7000 feet. It reaches its best growth in Washington, where it attains a height of 75 to 125 feet and a diameter of 2 to 5 feet.

Form. The branches are pendulous, giving the tree a " weeping " form; the crown is open and narrowly pyramidal; the stem is tapering and clear of branches for one third to one half the total height. The spire-like leader bends over gracefully. Frequently the stem is buttressed.

Occurrence. The yellow cedar prefers the deep, moist, open soils of river, valley, and cañon bottoms, but is often found on northern and western slopes and on benches and table-lands. It occurs singly or in small groups and is associated with spruce, fir, hemlock, other cedars, and the hardwoods.

Distinctive characteristics. The yellow cedar may be distinguished by (1) the small, sharp, harsh, scale-like, blue-green leaves; (2) the drooping, flat sprays; (3) the small ($\frac{1}{4}$ to $\frac{1}{2}$ inch), globose, reddish-brown cones covered with a white powder; and (4) the thin ($\frac{1}{2}$ inch), ashy-brown (red-brown inside) bark broken into narrow ridges by shallow fissures and flaking off in long strips.

Wood. The wood is light, soft, rather brittle, weak, fine-grained, splits easily, but is exceedingly durable; it seasons well, is easily worked, and takes a fine polish. The heartwood is a clear sulphur-yellow; the sapwood is thin and white. The wood possesses a distinctive odor.

Uses. Yellow cedar is used for general construction, interior finishing, shingles, poles, fencing, and foundation blocks. Its use is limited, however, by the restricted distribution.

The yellow cedar is of value for park and yard plantings, especially in group plantings of the lighter-foliaged evergreens. It is used for ornamental purposes in Europe.

PORT ORFORD CEDAR, WHITE CEDAR, OR LAWSON'S CYPRESS

(*Chamæcyparis lawsoniana*)

The Port Orford cedar has a very restricted distribution in the coast region of southern Oregon and northern California, extending inland only about forty miles. Its altitudinal range is from sea level to 5000 feet. It reaches its best development in the vicinity of the ocean shore, where it attains a height of 100 to 200 feet and a diameter of 3 to 8 feet.

Form. The young tree has a dense, pyramidal crown of small, pendulous, rather feathery branches which persist to a point near the ground. Mature forest-grown trees develop a long, straight, cylindrical, clear stem, rising from a broadly buttressed base, and a pyramidal crown comprising one third to one half the total height of the tree. The root system is spreading.

Occurrence. Port Orford cedar is not exacting as to soil requirements but thrives best in a deep, open, moderately moist soil. It seldom occurs in a pure stand and is usually associated with the other cedars, spruce, fir, hemlock, sugar pine, and redwood.

Distinctive characteristics. The Port Orford cedar may be distinguished by (1) the soft, minute, yellow-green leaves and flattened twigs and branching; (2) the small, berry-like, russet (when mature) cones; (3) the

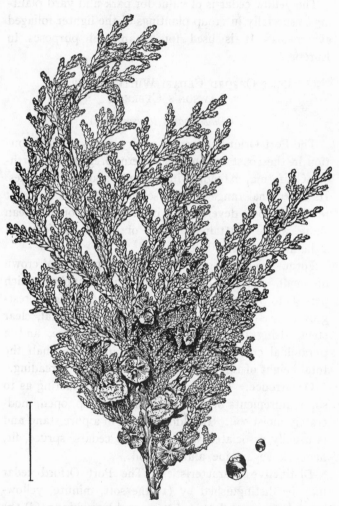

Fig. 48. Port Orford cedar. Branch showing cones; and two seeds, one natural size and the other twice natural size.

thick, cinnamon-brown bark divided into long, narrow, loose, rather stringy ridges by deep fissures; and (4) the pendulous, feathery branching of young trees.

Wood. The wood is light, soft to moderately hard, strong for its weight, of close texture, shows no pronounced grain, and is extremely durable; it seasons well, is easily worked, and takes a fine polish. The wood possesses a distinctive odor which is very strong when freshly cut. The heartwood is pale yellow or brownish; the sapwood is white. In general appearance the wood resembles white pine.

Uses. Port Orford cedar is used for general construction, bridge timbers, poles, shingles, interior finishing, and packing boxes. The usefulness of the wood is limited by the restricted range.

The Port Orford cedar is extensively used for ornamental purposes, both in the United States and in Europe. Open-grown park specimens are greatly admired for the graceful form and striking beauty of the fine branching.

RED CEDAR[1]

(*Thuja plicata*)

Red cedar is found at elevations of 1000 to 7500 feet in a range that extends throughout the northern part of the Rocky Mountain system, from Montana westward to Washington and southward to central California and Colorado. It reaches its best develop-

---

[1] The red cedar is not a true cedar (*Chamæcyparis*); it is more closely related to the arbor vitæs (*Thuja*) than to the cedars, but it is known in almost every section as " cedar."

ment in Washington and Oregon, where it attains a height of 100 to 200 feet and a diameter of 4 to (occasionally) 15 feet.

Form. The stem tapers rapidly from a buttressed, fluted base, and rises straight, cylindrical, and clear of branches for one half or more of the total height; the crown is densely pyramidal, spire-pointed, and composed of small branches. As the trees grow older the crown gradually becomes open and rounded. The root system is spreading.

Occurrence. The red cedar thrives best in the moist, deep, open soils of river bottoms, lower slopes, benches, and about mountain meadows. Occasionally it occurs in small pure groups but usually it is found in mixture with spruce, hemlock, fir, white pine, larch, Douglas fir, redwood, and the hardwoods.

Distinctive characteristics. The red cedar may be distinguished by (1) the scale-like, opposite, soft, yellow-green leaves; (2) the flat branching; (3) the small ($\frac{1}{2}$ to $\frac{3}{4}$ inch) cones composed of six scales, each bearing either two or three seeds; and (4) the thin ($\frac{3}{4}$ inch), stringy, soft, cinnamon-brown (often grayish due to weathering) bark split into long continuous ridges by shallow fissures.

Wood. The wood is very soft, light, brittle, and weak, but has a straight grain, nails without splitting, and is very durable; it seasons well, is easily worked, and takes a fair polish. The heartwood is a dull grayish brown with a reddish tinge; the sapwood is thin and white. The wood possesses a peculiar aromatic, rather peppery, odor and taste which is distinctive.

FIG. 49.   Branch of red cedar, showing a cluster of open cones.
At the side are two of the small seeds.

Uses. Red cedar is used very extensively in the manufacture of shingles, and is in demand for telegraph and telephone poles. It is also used for general construction, siding and interior finishing, silo construction, and fencing.

The red cedar is a very graceful and beautiful tree. It is fairly resistant to drought and thrives in any deep, rather moist situation. Within its range it is frequently used for ornamental purposes.

Monterey Cypress

(*Cupressus macrocarpa*)

The Monterey cypress has a very limited distribution in the coastal region of central California, where it attains a height of 40 to 60 feet and a diameter of 1 to 2 feet.

Form. The crown of the young tree is conical, the branches extending to the ground. (See Figure 6.) With age the lateral branches develop upward until the crown is broad and flattened above and bush-like below. In the forest-grown tree the stem is rather irregular, tapering, and clear of branches for perhaps one fourth the total height. The root system is deep and spreading.

Occurrence. The Monterey cypress thrives best in a deep, moist, open, well-drained soil in the vicinity of the ocean, where it mingles with pine and the hardwoods. It frequently occurs in extensive open, pure stands.

Distinctive characteristics. The Monterey cypress may be distinguished by (1) the broad, flat, bush-like

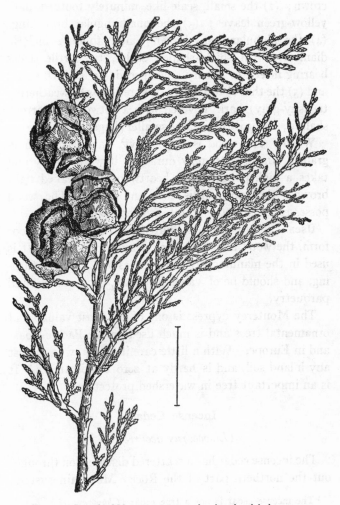

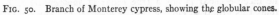

FIG. 50. Branch of Monterey cypress, showing the globular cones.

crown; (2) the small, scale-like, minutely toothed, dark yellow-green leaves; (3) the quadrangular branching; (4) the globular, ashy-brown cones, about 1 inch in diameter, with shield-shaped scales, the fertile scales bearing fifteen to twenty angled seeds under each scale; and (5) the thin ($\frac{1}{2}$ to 1 inch), deep red-brown (weathering to ashy-gray) bark, covered with a network of narrow, shallow, vertical ridges and smaller diagonal ridges.

Wood. The wood is very heavy, hard, strong, fine-grained, and is extremely durable; it works easily and takes a high polish. The heartwood is streaked light brown; the sapwood is thin and white. The wood possesses a distinctive, faint, aromatic odor.

Uses. Because of its limited distribution and poor form, the wood is not of great commercial value. It is used in the manufacture of novelties and in wood turning, and should be of value for inlay, cabinetwork, and parquetry.

The Monterey cypress is one of the most valuable of ornamental trees and is much used on the Pacific Coast and in Europe. With a little care it will grow in almost any inland soil, and is hardy at zero temperatures. It is an important tree in watershed protection.

Incense Cedar [1]

(*Libocedrus decurrens*)

The incense cedar has a scattered distribution throughout the northern part of the Rocky Mountain system,

---

[1] The incense cedar is not a true cedar (*Chamæcyparis*), but it resembles this group so closely that it goes by the name "cedar" wherever it is found.

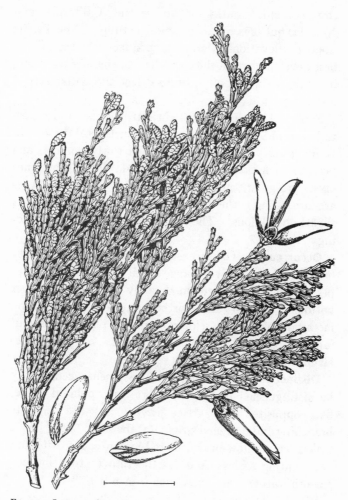

FIG. 51. Incense cedar. At the left is a branch containing staminate flowers; at the right is a fruiting branch, showing the peculiar two-scaled cone. Below are two seeds.

from Canada southward to central California and Nevada, but it is confined almost entirely to the Pacific slope, at elevations of 2000 to 7000 feet. It reaches its best development on the west slope of the Sierras, where it attains a height of 150 to 200 feet and a diameter of 4 to 8 feet.

Form. The stem is straight, fairly clear, and tapers rather rapidly from a markedly buttressed base. In young trees the crown is open, narrowly conical, and persists to a point near the ground; later it becomes open, irregular, and rounded. The upper branches are ascending; the lower branches are horizontal or slightly pendulous. The root system is deep and spreading.

Occurrence. The incense cedar thrives on a variety of soils and under a wide range of soil moisture. It grows best in the deep, open, moderately moist soil of river bottoms, western and northern slopes, benches, and mountain parks. It seldom occurs in pure stands, but is associated with sugar pine, yellow pine, big tree, Douglas fir, and a few hardwoods.

Distinctive characteristics. The incense cedar may be distinguished by (1) the short, soft, pointed, scale-like, opposite bright-green leaves; (2) the opposite branching and flattened twigs; (3) the small ($\frac{1}{2}$ to $\frac{3}{4}$ inch), cylindrical, yellow-brown to red-brown cones, with but two fruiting scales; and (4) the thin (1 to 3 inches), smooth, rather scaly, cinnamon-brown bark.

Wood. The wood is soft, light, weak, brittle, has an aromatic odor and spicy flavor, but is very durable; it seasons well, is easily worked, but is frequently found

to be defective (pecky). The heartwood is a dull yellowish brown with a reddish tinge; the sapwood is thin
and pale yellow.

Uses. Incense cedar is used for general construction,
shingles, telegraph and telephone poles, and fencing.
The wood is of a lower commercial value than that of
any of the trees with which it is associated.

The incense cedar is occasionally used for ornamental
purposes. Seedlings are easily produced and thrive in
almost any situation.

Big Tree or Sequoia
(*Sequoia gigantea*)

The big tree is of ancient origin. Fossil remains of
its ancestors have been found in pre-glacial deposits in
the Arctic regions — its habitat at that time. Today it
has a very limited distribution. It is found only in
central California, occurring at elevations of 5000 to
8000 feet. It is without doubt the largest and most
magnificent tree of America. Occasionally it attains a
height of 325 feet and a diameter of 25 feet.

Form. The stem is straight, columnar, and clear of
branches for a great height; the base is markedly buttressed; the crown is flat, irregular, and is composed of
a few large branches. In young trees the crown consists of small branches which persist to a point near the
ground, giving the tree a roundly pyramidal shape.

Occurrence. The big tree thrives best in a deep,
moist, open, well-drained soil and occupies the depres-
sions and slopes about the headwaters of streams. Occasionally it occurs in a pure stand, but usually it is

associated with sugar pine, yellow pine, Douglas fir, white fir, and incense cedar.

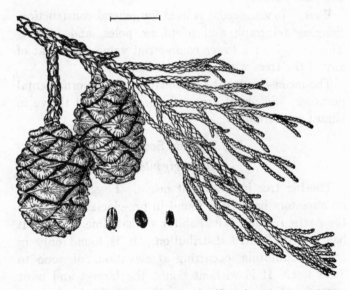

FIG. 52. Branch of the big tree, showing the oblong, hanging cones and the shield-shaped scales. Below are a few of the seeds.

Distinctive characteristics. The big tree may be distinguished by (1) the short, sharp-pointed, scale-like, blue-green needles, resembling the cedars; (2) the oblong cones about 2 inches long, with shield-shaped scales, each covering from four to six angular seeds; (3) the thin, grayish, unbroken bark of young stems and branches; and (4) the thick (12 to 18 inches), soft, spongy, fibrous, cinnamon-red bark of old stems, broken into large ridges by deep fissures.

Wood. The wood is soft, light, weak, brittle, has a coarse but indistinct grain, splits easily, and is very durable; it is easily worked and takes a good polish. The heartwood is a dull purplish red-brown; the sapwood is thin and white.

Uses. The wood of the big tree is marketed under the trade name of " redwood " and is used for the same general purposes as redwood (see page 61). Most of the remaining stands of big tree have been placed in federal and state parks and are under protection.

Both the bark and the wood contain a high percentage of tannic acid.

California Nutmeg or Stinking Cedar[*]
(*Tumion californicum*)

The California nutmeg, so called because of the resemblance of the seed to the nutmeg of commerce, has a general distribution throughout central California, at elevations of 2000 to 6000 feet. It reaches its best development in the northern coast ranges, where it attains a height of 50 to 100 feet and a diameter of 1 to 3 feet.

Form. The stem of the forest tree is more or less crooked, tapering, and clear of branches for less than one fourth the total height; the crown is rounded and dome-like. The crown of the sapling is pyramidal and composed of small, horizontal or slightly pendulous branches. The root system is spreading.

Occurrence. The California nutmeg thrives best in the deep, moist, open soils of sheltered cañons and stream bottoms, where it occurs in small pure stands or is associated with maple, alder, sycamore, and the willows. In the drier situations the growth is shrubby.

---

[*] The leaves of this species are needle-like, not scale-like as is incorrectly implied by its inclusion in this part of the present work.

Distinctive characteristics. The California nutmeg may be distinguished by (1) the disagreeable aromatic

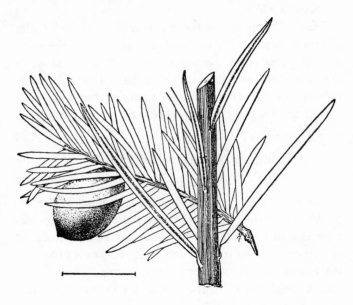

FIG. 53.   Branch and plum-like fruit of the California nutmeg.

odor of the crushed leaves and bark; (2) the long (1 to 3 inches), flat, sharp-pointed, glossy, deep yellow-green leaves; (3) the large (1 to 1½ inches), light-green or pur-plish, plum-like fruit containing the large seed; (4) the thin (about ½ inch), rather soft, scaly, grayish-brown bark of old stems, broken into narrow ridges by deep fissures and narrow cross seams; and (5) the attractive green foliage and symmetrical crown.

Wood. The wood is heavy, hard, strong, dense, of uniform texture, and durable; it seasons poorly, but is moderately easy to work and takes a fine finish. The heartwood is a lemon-yellow; the sapwood is thin and nearly white. The wood is slightly aromatic.

Uses. Because of the small supply, the wood has little commercial value. Occasionally it is used for cabinetwork, wood turning, and in making novelties. Locally it is used for fencing.

The California nutmeg is an attractive ornamental tree; it is occasionally planted throughout its natural range and also in Europe.

Yew*

(*Taxus brevifolia*)

The yew has a general distribution throughout the Rocky Mountains, from Canada southward to central California and Utah, at elevations of 1000 to 6000 feet. It reaches its best development on the western slopes of the Cascade Range, where it attains a height of 20 to 80 feet and a diameter of 12 to 30 inches.

Form. The crown is open and narrowly conical, the small branches extending to a point near the ground in the sapling stage. In older trees the stem is tapering, straight, markedly fluted, and clear for about one fourth the total height; the crown is open and pyramidal. The lower branches are inclined to droop, giving the tree a " weeping " appearance.

Occurrence. The yew thrives best in a deep, open, well-drained soil and is found at its best in cañon bottoms and along streams. Frequently, however, it is found in rather dry situations, where it is associated with Douglas fir, redwood, and the hardwoods.

* The leaves of this species are needle-like, not scale-like as is incorrectly implied by its inclusion in this part of the present work.

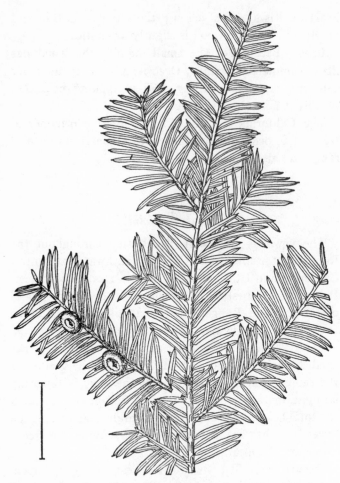

Fig. 54. **Yew.** Note the flat, pointed needles and the small button-like fruit.

Distinctive characteristics. The yew may be distinguished by (1) the sharp-pointed, flat, deep yellow-green leaves; (2) the flattened twigs; (3) the small, red, rounded, flattened fruit and the hard seed; and (4) the thin, purple-red bark covered with papery, purple scales which break away easily.

Wood. The wood is light, close-grained, moderately heavy, elastic, medium strong, of uniform texture, and very durable; it seasons fairly well, is easily worked, and takes a high polish. The heartwood is a clear rose-red; the sapwood is thin and white.

Uses. Yew is in demand by the manufacturers of canoe paddles, novelties, and bows, and for cabinetwork and wood turning. Its utilization is limited by its small size and its scarcity.

The yew is frequently used in ornamental plantings and is much admired for the graceful form, the lustrous foliage, and the attractive red fruits. It is also useful for hedge and shelter-belt purposes.

The Junipers (*Juniperus*)

The junipers occur commonly at higher elevations and in the semi-arid regions, but seldom in commercial quantities. Because of the poor form (rapid taper and short stem) and their inaccessibility, the junipers are seldom manufactured. The wood is uniform in texture and very durable, and is in considerable demand for fencing purposes. In the semi-desert foothills they form a valuable protection cover.

The junipers are characterized by cherry-like fruits, consisting of a hard stone covered by a sweetish pulp. The leaves are scale-like, sharp, and harsh to the touch. The bark is stringy.

KEY TO THE JUNIPERS

A. Bark red-brown; fruit containing
   2 or 3 seeds . . . . JUNIPER (*J. occidentalis*)
B. Bark gray-brown; fruit containing
   1 seed . . . . ONE-SEED JUNIPER
   (*J. monosperma*)

JUNIPER OR CEDAR

(*Juniperus occidentalis*)

The juniper has a general distribution throughout the Rocky Mountain system, from Canada southward to the Mexican border, at elevations of 500 feet in the northern part of its range to 11,000 feet in the southern part. It reaches its best development in the mountain cañons of the Sierra Nevadas, where it attains a height of 20 to 60 feet and a diameter of 2 to 6 feet.

Form. In the sapling stage the crown is narrowly conical and composed of many small branches which persist to a point near the ground. In the mature tree the stem tapers rapidly and is usually clear for but a few feet; the crown is broadly rounded, open, and composed of several large branches. The root system is wide-spreading.

Occurrence. The juniper thrives best in a deep, open, moderately moist soil; but it occurs more frequently in the drier, open, stony soils of the high slopes and ridges. It forms extensive open stands, but occasionally mingles with Jeffrey pine, fir, and spruce.

Distinctive characteristics. The juniper may be distinguished by (1) the short, tapering stem and spreading crown; (2) the blue-black berries, covered with a

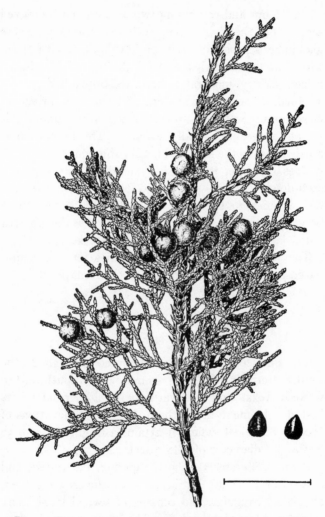

FIG. 55. Branch of juniper, showing the cherry-like fruits. At the right
are two seeds.

white bloom and containing two or three hard, grooved seeds; (3) the light-green, scale-like leaves with the glandular deposits of resin on the back, occurring in three's about the twig; and (4) the thin ($\frac{1}{2}$ to 1 inch), ridged, stringy, moderately hard, red-brown bark.

Wood. The wood is moderately hard, light, brittle, of close texture, slightly aromatic, and very durable; it seasons well and is easily worked. The heartwood is a pale brown; the sapwood is thin and white.

Uses. Juniper is extensively used for fencing in the semi-desert country. It is also used for fuel, although it is inferior to the pines. The United States Forest Service recommends it as a substitute for the Eastern red cedar in the production of pencil stock.

The juniper holds some possibilities for ornamental purposes in the planting of dry, rocky situations.

ONE-SEED JUNIPER

(*Juniperus monosperma*)

The one-seed juniper is distributed throughout the southwestern United States, from Colorado southward to western Texas and westward to Nevada, reaching its best development in northern Arizona at elevations of 6000 to 8000 feet, where it attains a height of 40 to 50 feet and a diameter of 1 to 3 feet.

Form. The stem is short, tapering, buttressed, and clear of branches for but a few feet; the crown is open, spreading, irregular, and consists of several large, more or less contorted branches. The root system is deep and spreading.

Occurrence. The one-seed juniper occupies the semi-desert foothills, where it forms extensive pure stands or occurs in mixture with the piñon pines and mountain mahogany. It thrives best in the deep, open, sandy, gravelly soils where the level of ground water lies at a depth of 20 or more feet.

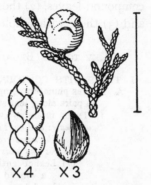

×4 ×3

Fig. 56. One-seed juniper. Above, twig and fruit, natural size. Below, at the left, tip of a twig, magnified four times, at the right, a seed magnified three times.

Distinctive characteristics. The one-seed juniper may be distinguished by (1) the bushy, irregular form; (2) the sharp, pointed, gray-green, scaly leaves of leading shoots, arranged in three's about the twig; (3) the soft, short, thickened, gray-green scale leaves of the lateral twigs; (4) the large ($\frac{1}{4}$ inch), fleshy, dark-blue or copper-colored berries, covered with a white powder and containing a single seed (rarely two or three); and (5) the thin, ashy-gray or ashy-brown, fibrous bark of old stems, broken into long, connected, irregular, broad ridges.

Wood. The wood is moderately heavy, hard, brittle, dense, of uniform texture, and durable; it seasons well, works easily, and takes a fine finish. The heartwood is a light red-brown; the sapwood is thin and pale brown.

Uses. One-seed juniper is utilized extensively in the production of fencing material and is of inestimable value in the prevention of wind erosion.

PART II. THE BROADLEAF TREES

THE broadleaf trees, or hardwoods, are divided into three groups for purposes of description: (1) those with compound leaves, (2) those with lobed or divided leaves, and (3) those with simple leaves.

KEY TO THE BROADLEAF (HARDWOOD) TREES

I. TREES WITH COMPOUND LEAVES
  A. **Leaves pinnately compound (leaflets in pairs along leaf stem)**
    1. TWIGS UNARMED (WITHOUT THORNS)
      a. Leaves and buds alternate; pith chambered . . . . . WALNUTS (*Juglans*)
      b. Leaves and buds opposite; pith solid
        (1) Leaflets entire; fruit a winged seed . . OREGON ASH (*Fraxinus*)
        (2) Leaflets toothed; fruit cherry-like . . . . . ELDER (*Sambucus*)
    2. TWIGS ARMED (THORNS PRESENT)
      a. Leaves singly compound . BLACK LOCUST (*Robinia*)
      b. Leaves doubly compound . . MESQUITES (*Prosopis*)
  B. **Leaves palmately compound** . . **(leaflets radiating from end of leaf stem)** . . . . CALIFORNIA BUCKEYE (*Æsculus*)

II. TREES WITH LOBED OR DIVIDED LEAVES
  A. **Leaves and buds opposite; fruit winged** . . . . . . BROADLEAF MAPLE (*Acer*)
  B. **Leaves and buds alternate; fruit not winged**
    1. FRUIT AN ACORN; BARK OF BRANCHES DARK-COLORED . . WHITE OAKS (*Quercus*)
    2. FRUIT BALL-LIKE; BARK OF BRANCHES CREAMY . . . . SYCAMORES (*Platanus*)

III. TREES WITH SIMPLE LEAVES
  A. **Leaves with toothed margin**
    1. LEAVES WITH IRREGULAR TEETH; FRUIT AN ACORN . LIVE OAKS (*Quercus*)
    2. LEAVES WITH REGULAR TEETH
      a. Leaves doubly toothed; fruit cone-like
        (1) Bark orange-brown, papery BIRCHES (*Betula*)
        (2) Bark grayish-white, tight . . ALDERS (*Alnus*)
      b. Leaves singly toothed; fruit not cone-like

    (1) Leaves coarsely toothed
      (a) Points of teeth sharp, bristle-tipped
        i. Fruit cherry-like SPANISH WILD CHERRY
                            (*Prunus*)
        ii. Fruit an acorn . BLACK OAKS (*Quercus*)
        iii. Fruit a prickly bur . . . CHINQUAPIN
                            (*Castanopsis*)
      (b) Points of teeth rounded, not harsh
        i. Fruit a catkin;
           seed cottony COTTONWOODS (*Populus*)
    (2) Leaves finely toothed
      (a) Leaves long, nar-
         row, lance-like . BLACK WILLOW (*Salix*)
      (b) Leaves oblong or round
        i. Fruit cherry-like
          (*i*) Fruit in clusters . BITTER CHERRY
                            (*Prunus*)
          (*ii*) Fruit singly in
             axils of leaves HACKBERRIES (*Celtis*)
        ii. Fruit a catkin;
           seed cottony . . . ASPEN (*Populus*)

B. Leaves with smooth margin (entire)

  1. LEAVES LONG, NARROW, LANCE-LIKE
    a. Bark brown, scaly; fruit a
      round pod . . . . DESERT WILLOW (*Chilopsis*)
    b. Bark grayish, tight; fruit
      a tailed seed . . . . . MOUNTAIN MAHOGANY
                         (*Cercocarpus*)
  2. LEAVES SICKLE-SHAPED, LANCE-LIKE, LEATHERY
    a. Bark scaly, ridged or peeling . GUMS (*Eucalyptus*)
  3. LEAVES OBLONG TO ROUNDED
    a. Leaves deciduous, thin, not leathery
      (1) Fruit cherry-like
        (a) Fruit borne in axils of leaves . BEARBERRY
                            (*Rhamnus*)
        (b) Fruit borne in
          terminal heads . . DOGWOOD (*Cornus*)
    b. Leaves persistent, thick, leathery
      (1) Bark of young stems and branches scaly,
        dark brown; fruit olive-like, in leaf
        axils CALIFORNIA LAUREL (*Umbellularia*)
      (2) Bark of young stems and branches smooth,
        red; fruit cherry-like in terminal clusters
                    MADROÑAS (*Arbutus*)

SECTION 1. TREES WITH COMPOUND LEAVES

WALNUTS   BLACK LOCUST
OREGON ASH   MESQUITES
ELDER   CALIFORNIA BUCKEYE

The Walnuts (*Juglans*)

KEY TO THE WALNUTS

A. Leaflets 9 to 23; nut deeply grooved . . . . . . WALNUT
(*J. rupestris*)
B. Leaflets 11 to 17; nut obscurely grooved CALIFORNIA WALNUT
(*J. californica*)

WALNUT

(*Juglans rupestris*)

The walnut is distributed throughout the southwestern United States from Texas westward to eastern California and southward into Mexico, occurring at elevations of 1000 to 6000 feet.   Under favorable conditions it attains a height of 50 to 60 feet and a diameter of 3 to 5 feet.

Form.   In the open the stem is short, straight, and cylindrical, usually dividing at a height of 10 to 15 feet into several large branches; the crown is broad and rounded.   In rather dry situations the growth is shrubby.

Occurrence.   The walnut occupies the cañon bottoms and margins of streams, occasionally growing on northern slopes.   It never occurs in pure stands, but is associated with birch, willow, sycamore, cottonwood, and the oaks.   The root system is deep and spreading.

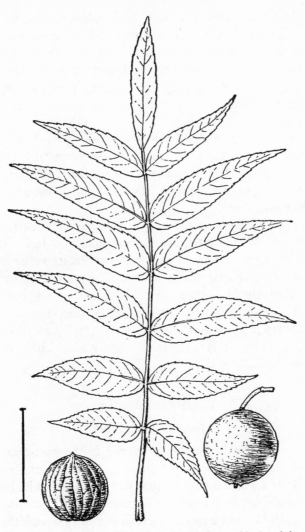

FIG. 57. Leaf and fruit of the walnut, showing the round husk and the
characteristic grooved nut.

Distinctive characteristics. The walnut may be distinguished by (1) the large, compound, yellow-green leaves; (2) the male flowers in yellowish catkins; (3) the round, velvety fruit with the thin husk and smoothly grooved nut; (4) the moderately thick ($\frac{1}{2}$ to 1 inch), deeply ridged, whitish bark, broken into thin scales on the surface.

Wood. The wood is moderately heavy, hard, strong, close-grained, and very durable; it seasons fairly well, is easily worked, and takes a fine polish. The heartwood is purplish brown; the sapwood is moderately thick and white.

Uses. Walnut is used for farm repairs, cabinetmaking, interior finishing, fencing material, and fuel. Because of the dearth of hardwood within its range and the difficulties of transportation, the walnut occupies a relatively important place.

The walnut is used for ornamental purposes in the southern and eastern United States and also in Europe, where it is considered superior to the larger growing Eastern tree.

CALIFORNIA WALNUT

(*Juglans californica*)

The California walnut is confined to the west-central and southern portions of California, occurring at elevations of a few hundred to 4000 feet. It reaches its best development in the stream bottoms, where it attains a height of 40 to 60 feet and a diameter of 15 to 20 inches.

Form. The stem is straight, cylindrical, and clear of

branches for one third to one half the total height; the
crown is full and rounded. In the open the stem splits
into several large branches at a height of 6 or 8 feet.
The root system is deep and spreading.

Occurrence. The California walnut thrives best in
the deep, moist, open, sandy or gravelly soils of stream
bottoms, where it is associated with the oaks and other
moisture-loving hardwoods. It seldom occurs in pure
stands.

Distinctive characteristics. The California walnut
may be distinguished by (1) the compound leaves composed of from eleven to seventeen oval, toothed leaflets;
(2) the reddish-brown, hairy twigs; (3) the small (1 to
$1\frac{1}{4}$ inches), round fruit containing the obscurely grooved
nut; (4) the smooth, pale-gray bark of young stems and
branches; (5) the dark-brown, irregularly ridged bark
of old stems; and (6) the chambered pith of twigs.

Wood. The wood is moderately heavy, hard, medium
strong, uniform in texture, and durable; it seasons well,
works easily, and takes a fine finish. The heartwood is
dark brown; the sapwood is thin and pale brown.

Uses. California walnut is used for cabinetwork,
furniture, fencing materials, farm repairs, and fuel. It
is seldom of commercial size, and for this reason of no
great importance.

The walnut, with its associates, furnishes a growth of
considerable value for holding stream banks in the prevention of erosion.

Horticulturally the California walnut is used as a
stock upon which to graft or bud varieties of the English
walnut (*Juglans regia*), which is extensively grown in

the Southwest. It also possesses value as an ornamental tree and is frequently used in park and yard plantings.

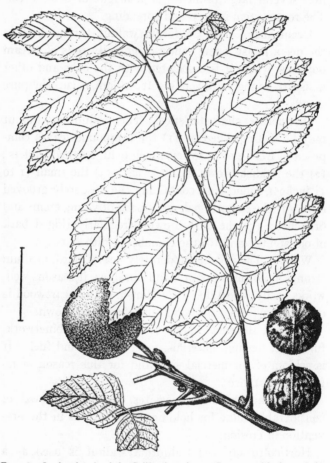

FIG. 58. Leaf and fruit of the California walnut. Compare with those of the other walnut (Fig. 57).

Oregon Ash

(*Fraxinus oregona*)

The Oregon ash is found commonly throughout the Pacific Coast region, from Canada southward to the Mexican border, occurring at various elevations from sea level to about 5000 feet. It reaches its best development in western Oregon, where it attains a height of 60 to 80 feet and a diameter of 2 to 4 feet.

Form. The stem of the forest-grown tree is long, straight, cylindrical, and clear of branches for one half to two thirds the total height; the crown is narrow, short, rounded, and composed of small, rather coarse branches. In the open the crown is spreading and rounded and the stem is short and thick. The root system is deep and spreading.

Occurrence. The Oregon ash thrives best in the deep, moist, open, well-drained, fertile soils of river bottoms, stream banks, moist benches, and mountain valleys, where it is associated with alder, maple, sycamore, fir, oak, and cottonwood. In dry situations the growth is shrubby. It seldom occurs in a pure stand.

Distinctive characteristics. The Oregon ash may be distinguished by (1) the opposite branching; (2) the large compound leaves, composed of seven to nine entire or indistinctly toothed, light-green leaflets; (3) the orange-colored, more or less hairy, round twigs, flattened at the buds; (4) the large clusters of single-winged fruits; (5) the soft, dark grayish-brown bark of old stems, broken into broad ridges by narrow fissures and cross fissures; and (6) the rather coarse, upright branches.

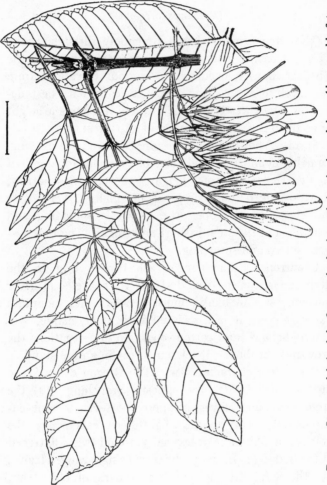

Fig. 59.   Leaves and fruit of the Oregon ash, showing variations in size and shape of leaves and leaflets.

Wood. The wood is fairly heavy, hard, strong, rather brittle, somewhat coarse-grained, moderately elastic, but not durable; it seasons well, is easily worked, and takes a fine finish. The heartwood is a light yellow brown; the sapwood is thick and pale yellow.

Uses. Oregon ash is used for handles, farm repairs, wagon stock, agricultural implements, interior finishing, flooring, furniture, cooperage, general construction, and fuel. It is somewhat inferior to the Eastern ashes, but is used for the same purposes.

The Oregon ash is a beautiful ornamental tree and is extensively planted for park, yard, and street purposes. When once established, it thrives in dry situations.

Elder or Elderberry
(*Sambucus glauca*)

The elder has a general distribution throughout the Pacific Coast states from Canada southward to the Mexican border and eastward into Montana, Utah, and Arizona, occurring at various elevations from sea level to 6000 feet. It reaches its best development in western Oregon, where it attains a height of 30 to 50 feet and a diameter of 1 to 2 feet.

Form. The stem is long, straight, rather buttressed at the base, and clear of branches for one half the total height; the crown is flat, rounded, and consists of coarse, crooked branches. At higher elevations the growth is quite shrubby. The root system is spreading.

Occurrence. The elder thrives best in the deep, moist, open, sandy or gravelly, well-drained soils of cañon and valley bottoms; also on stream banks and about springs and seeps. It is usually associated with maple, alder, madroña, yellow pine, sugar pine, Douglas fir, and the

Fig. 60. Leaves and fruit cluster of the elder.

oaks. Occasionally it occurs as a dense, shrubby growth marking the course of a stream.

Distinctive characteristics. The elder may be distinguished by (1) the coarse, hairy, reddish-brown, rather angular twigs, which have a large pith; (2) the stout, weed-like growth of the compound leaves, which are composed of from three to nine oblong, lance-like, finely toothed leaflets, bluish green on the upper side and pale green on the lower side; (3) the flat, terminal head (cyme) of minute yellow flowers; (4) the clusters of juicy, sweet, blue-black, cherry-like fruits, covered with a whitish powder which rubs off easily; (5) the thin, yellow-brown bark of old stems, broken into a network of connected, narrow ridges by shallow fissures.

Wood. The wood is light, soft, weak, brittle, and not durable; it seasons well and works easily. The heartwood is a pale brownish yellow; the sapwood is thick and white.

Uses. The wood of the elder is of little value for industrial purposes. It is used locally for fuel.

As a large-growing shrub, the elder is an attractive ornamental tree. In group plantings the clusters of fruit may be gathered and utilized. It is easily transplanted and stands handling well.

Black Locust, Common Locust, or Yellow Locust
(*Robinia pseudacacia*)

The black locust, or locust, has been naturalized over the entire United States and southern Canada. In the West, it frequently attains a height of 60 to 80 feet and a diameter of 24 to 30 inches.

Form. The crown is open and the branches long, spreading, and graceful. In the forest the stem is long, straight, cylindrical, and clear of branches. In the shelter belt it stands cutting back and sprouts prolifically.

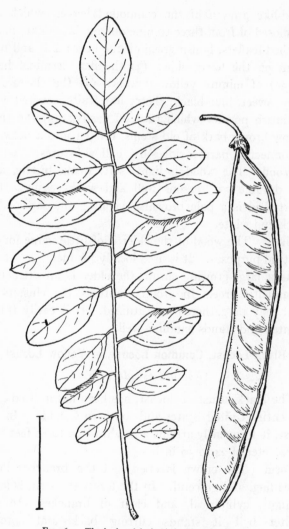

Fig. 61. The leaf and fruit of the black locust.

Occurrence. The locust makes its best growth on the deep, rich, moist, well-drained soils of river bottoms and northern slopes. Once it secures a footing, however, it will maintain itself anywhere, although the growth is, of course, very slow in dry situations. Usually it is associated with ash, hickory, maple, poplar, and elm.

Distinctive characteristics. The locust may be distinguished by (1) the short bark-thorns (similar to those on a rosebush) at the base of the leaf petiole (stem); (2) the compound leaves (the leaflets are much larger than those of the honey locust); (3) the clusters of white, pea-like flowers in the early spring; (4) the scaly, ridged bark; and (5) the papery pods inclosing the small, hard, dark-colored seed.

Wood. The wood of the locust is heavy, hard, strong, fairly elastic, and very durable; it is rather difficult to season and to work. The heartwood is dark brown; the sapwood is thick or thin and light-colored; pith rays are visible, but are rather indistinct.

Uses. Because of the durable character of the wood, its rapidity of growth, and ease of propagation, locust is primarily a fence-post tree. The wood is also used as wagon stock, in shipbuilding, in making novelties by wood turning, and in the manufacture of brackets (insulating) and agricultural implements and vehicles. As it is liable to attack by the locust borer, the wood is often of no value for saw purposes.

The locust tree is very graceful, approaching the elm in form, and is much used in large plantings. Occasionally it is planted along streets, giving entire satisfaction. As a hedge plant or shelter-belt tree on the farm, it stands cutting back and reproduces readily from sprouts.

The Mesquites (*Prosopis*)

KEY TO THE MESQUITES

A. **Bark light-brown with long, ribbon-like scales** . . . . SCREW BEAN (*P. odorata*)
B. **Bark dark-reddish brown with short, thick scales** . . . . MESQUITE (*P. juliflora*)

SCREW BEAN OR SCREW-POD MESQUITE

(*Prosopis odorata*)

The screw bean is distributed throughout the southern Rocky Mountain system from Colorado, Utah, and Nevada to the Mexican border, occurring at elevations of 3000 to 6000 feet. It reaches its best development in Arizona, where it attains a height of 25 to 30 feet and a diameter of 12 to 15 inches.

Form. The stem is short, more or less crooked, and clear of branches for but a few feet above ground, the crown is dense, irregularly rounded, and spreading. Usually the form is quite shrubby. The root system is deep and spreading.

Occurrence. The screw bean thrives best in the deep, open, sandy soils of the desert river bottoms and cañons, where it frequently occurs in nearly pure stands. Occasionally it is found in mixture with the desert junipers and the piñon pines.

Distinctive characteristics. The screw bean may be distinguished by (1) the doubly compound leaves, composed of small, oblong, grayish-green leaflets; (2) the sharp, woody thorns at the base of the leaf stem; (3) the yellow, spirally twisted pod containing ten to twenty small, hard seeds; and (4) the thick, light-brown bark of old stems, separating into long, ribbon-like scales.

FIG. 62.   Branch and fruit of the screw bean, showing the characteristic spirally twisted pods.

Wood. The wood is heavy, hard, close-grained, of uniform texture, dense, and durable; it seasons badly, checks, is difficult to work, but takes a fine finish. The heartwood is a pale yellowish brown; the sapwood is thin and pale yellow.

Uses. Screw bean is an exceedingly valuable fuel wood. It is also used for fencing purposes where it is of sufficient size, and is of considerable value for farm repairs.

The tree is browsed by all classes of grazing animals, and the fruit at least is believed to have considerable forage value.

The screw bean may be retained or transplanted about ranch buildings; the effect in these situations is quite pleasing. Within its range it has some ornamental value, more especially in the drier situations.

MESQUITE OR HONEY LOCUST

(*Prosopis juliflora*)

The mesquite occurs commonly throughout the southern Rocky Mountains from Colorado, Utah, and Nevada southward to the Mexican border, occurring at elevations of 4000 to 6000 feet. It reaches its best development in Arizona, where it attains a height of 30 to 40 feet and a diameter of 1 to 2 feet.

Form. The stem is rather short, more or less crooked, and clear of branches for less than one fourth the total height; the crown is rounded and spreading. Frequently the growth is very shrubby. The taproot penetrates deeply into the earth.

Occurrence. The mesquite thrives in the deep, open, sandy soils of the desert valleys and low foothills of the mountains. It occurs in extensive pure stands or in

FIG. 63. Branch and fruit of the mesquite.

mixture with the desert junipers, piñon pines, screw bean, and the Spanish bayonet.

Distinctive characteristics. The mesquite may be distinguished by (1) the doubly compound leaves, composed of small, oblong leaflets; (2) the long, woody, sharp thorns at the base of the leaf stems; (3) the clusters of long, flat to round pods which are markedly constricted between the hard, roundish seeds; and (4) the thick, dark reddish-brown bark of old stems, broken into short, thick scales by shallow fissures.

Wood. The wood is heavy, hard, strong, tough, close-grained, of uniform texture, and durable; it seasons poorly, is difficult to work, but takes a fine finish. The heartwood is a rich reddish brown; the sapwood is thin and pale brown.

Uses. Mesquite is used for fencing materials, crossties, rough construction, furniture, wagon stock, ranch repairs, paving blocks, fuel, and charcoal. Its use is limited by the poor form and small amount of merchantable material.

Both wood and bark contain a high percentage of tannin, which will undoubtedly open up a new market for the tree in the future. A gum which exudes from wounds is used as a substitute for gum arabic. The fruit is used as an article of diet by the Indians and is also much relished by all classes of grazing animals.

California Buckeye or Horse Chestnut
(*Æsculus californica*)

The California buckeye has a general distribution throughout central and southern California, occurring at various elevations from sea level to 5000 feet. Under favorable conditions it attains a height of 30 to 40 feet and a diameter of 1 to 3 feet.

FIG. 64. Flowering spike, leaf, and pear-shaped fruit of the California buckeye.

Form. The stem is short, straight, buttressed, and clear of branches for less than one fourth the total height; the crown is spreading, rounded, and composed of large, horizontal branches. Under unfavorable conditions the growth is shrubby. The root system is spreading.

Occurrence. The California buckeye thrives best in the deep, moist, open soils of cañon bottoms and stream margins, where it is associated with the oaks, sycamore, and willows. In the drier situations it forms a part of the chaparral cover of the foothills.

Distinctive characteristics. The California buckeye may be distinguished by (1) the large, palmately compound, dark-green leaves, composed of five (four to seven) leaflets; (2) the large, smooth, pear-shaped fruit containing a single, smooth, chestnut-brown seed; (3) the large, resinous, scaly, dark-brown winter buds; (4) the thin, smooth, grayish-white bark of old stems; and (5) the short stem and rounded crown.

Wood. The wood is soft, light, brittle, of uniform texture, fine-grained, dents without splitting, and is not durable; it seasons well, is easily worked, and takes a fair finish. The heartwood is white or pale yellow; the sapwood is thick and white.

Uses. Because of its poor form and limited supply, the wood is not utilized commercially. It often furnishes summer fuel wood and treatment posts. Occasionally it is used in the manufacture of woodenware.

Buckeye is occasionally planted for ornamental purposes. The clusters of white or rose-colored blossoms in the early summer are especially attractive.

SECTION 2. TREES WITH LOBED OR DIVIDED LEAVES

BROADLEAF MAPLE   OAKS   SYCAMORES

Broadleaf Maple or Oregon Maple

(*Acer macrophyllum*)

The broadleaf maple occurs throughout the Pacific Coast region from Canada southward to the Mexican border, occurring at various elevations from sea level to 6000 feet.   It reaches its best development in western Oregon, where it attains a height of 80 to 100 feet and a diameter of 2 to 4 feet.

Form.   The stem of the forest-grown tree is long, straight, cylindrical, and clear of branches for one half to two thirds the total height; the crown is broadly rounded, symmetrical, and composed of numerous ascending branches.   In the open the stem is short and the crown full, rounded, and spreading.   (See Figure 3.) The root system is deep and spreading.

Occurrence.   The broadleaf maple thrives best in the deep, moist, open, alluvial soils of the river bottoms and narrow foothill valleys, where it forms extensive pure stands or occurs in mixture with laurel, lowland fir, sycamore, and the oaks.   In the drier situations the growth is poor.

Distinctive characteristics.   The broadleaf maple may be distinguished by (1) the large, firm, glossy, wavy-margined, star-shaped, dark-green leaves; (2) the fragrant yellow flowers which appear after the leaves are formed; (3) the clusters of hairy, tawny-yellow fruits, each fruit consisting of a double seed with attached wings; (4) the opposite branching of twigs; (5) the

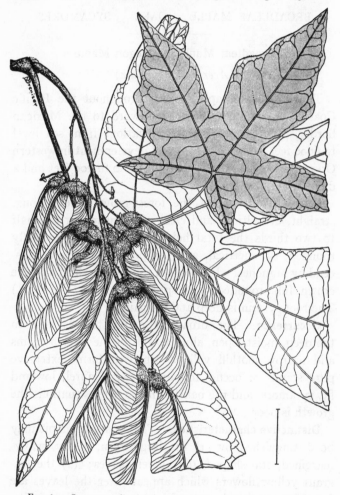

Fig. 65. Oregon maple, showing fruit cluster and two sizes of leaf.

thick, grayish-brown bark of old stems, broken into rough, hard, scaly ridges by shallow fissures; and (6) the dense, symmetrical, rounded crown.

Wood. The wood is moderately heavy, firm, medium strong, close-grained, of uniform texture, but not durable; it seasons well, works easily, and takes a fine finish. The heartwood is a light brown, tinged with red; the sapwood is thick and pale brown.

Uses. Broadleaf maple is used for general construction, furniture, interior finishing, office fixtures, handles, shipbuilding, wagon stock, farm repairs, and fuel. It is the most important hardwood timber tree of the region.

The broadleaf maple is a valuable ornamental tree and is widely planted for park, yard, and street purposes. The symmetrical crown and deep-green foliage are most attractive.

The Oaks (*Quercus*)

Of the twenty oaks occurring in the Western states, half the number may be said to possess at least local importance. As a matter of fact, even the scrub oaks furnish a forage in browse and mast which is of considerable value to the live-stock industry.

In general, the oaks are confined to the valley and cañon bottoms and the foothill slopes, forming an open, park-like stand of large trees. From the standpoint of lumber production the form is poor; yet, because of the dearth of hardwood timber, the product occupies a relatively important place in the industries. Usually there is a strong demand for fuel wood and much of the oak is cut for this purpose.

The oaks are characterized by (1) the clustering of the buds toward the ends of the twigs, (2) the star-shaped pith, (3) the acorn fruit, (4) the catkin male flower, and (5) the porous (usually markedly ring-porous) wood.

The oaks may be separated into two classes: (1) the live oaks, having persistent leaves; and (2) the deciduous oaks. The live oaks are characterized by relatively small, simple leaves with toothed or smooth margins. The deciduous oaks, characterized by lobed leaves, may be divided into two sub-groups: (a) the white oaks, having smooth, rounded lobes; and (b) the black oaks, having bristle-pointed lobes.

KEY TO THE OAKS

A. **Leaves divided or lobed**

    1. LOBES ROUNDED (WITHOUT BRISTLE POINTS)

        a. *Leaves yellow-green; bark dark gray-brown, deeply and broadly ridged* . . . . SCRUB OAK (*Q. gambelii*)

        b. *Leaves deep green; bark pale orange-brown, shallow-ridged* . . . PACIFIC POST OAK (*Q. garryana*)

        c. *Leaves dark green; bark light gray, deeply and broadly ridged* CALIFORNIA WHITE OAK (*Q. lobata*)

        d. *Leaves blue-green; bark pale brown, scaly* . . . . . . ROCK OAK (*Q. douglasii*)

    2. LOBES BRISTLE-POINTED . . . . CALIFORNIA BLACK OAK (*Q. californica*)

B. **Leaves not divided or lobed**

    1. LEAVES COARSELY TOOTHED (OCCASIONALLY ENTIRE), BRISTLE-POINTED

        a. *Leaves persistent, thick, leathery*

            (1) Leaves dark green . . . . HIGHLAND LIVE OAK (*Q. wislizeni*)

            (2) Leaves yellow-green . . . . . CAÑON LIVE OAK (*Q. chrysolepis*)

    b. Leaves deciduous
       (1) Leaves blue-green; bark
          pale brown, scaly . . . ROCK OAK (*Q. douglasii*)
       (2) Leaves light green; bark
          dark brown, broadly
          ridged . . . . . . CALIFORNIA LIVE OAK
                          (*Q. agrifolia*)

  2. LEAVES COARSELY TOOTHED, NOT BRISTLE-POINTED
    a. Leaves irregularly toothed, 1 to 5
       pairs of teeth . . . . . . EMORY OAK (*Q. emoryi*)
    b. Leaves regularly toothed . TANBARK OAK (*Q. densiflora*)

SCRUB OAK OR WHITE OAK
(*Quercus gambelii*)

The scrub oak is found commonly throughout the southern Rocky Mountains from Colorado westward to Nevada and southward to the Mexican border, occurring at elevations of 5000 to 10,000 feet. It reaches its best development in Utah, where it attains a height of 40 to 50 feet and a diameter of 12 to 18 inches.

Form. The stem is short, more or less crooked, and clear of branches for about one third the total height; the crown is narrow, rounded, and composed of numerous small, horizontal branches. In the drier situations the growth is very shrubby. The root system is deep and spreading.

Occurrence. The scrub oak thrives best in the deep, moist, open soils of the high mesas (plateaus) and upper slopes, where it occurs in extensive pure stands. Occasionally it is associated with the nut pines, Jeffrey pine, and the live oaks.

Distinctive characteristics. The scrub oak may be distinguished by (1) the oblong, deeply divided, round-lobed, dark yellow-green leaves, the undersides of which are lighter green and hairy; (2) the small, oval,

broad-based, dark chestnut-brown acorns, set one third in
the yellow-brown, scaly, hairy cups; (3) the orange-col-

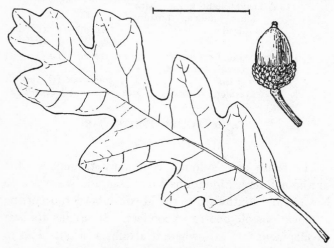

FIG. 66. Scrub oak. Compare the leaf and fruit with those of the Pacific post
oak (Fig. 67) and the California white oak (Fig. 68).

ored, hairy twigs of the current year; and (4) the moderately thick, grayish-brown bark of old stems, broken into
broad, flat, connecting ridges by shallow fissures.

Wood. The wood is heavy, hard, strong, tough, fine-
grained, of uniform texture, and durable; it seasons
poorly, is rather difficult to work, but takes a fine finish.
The heartwood is a dark reddish brown; the sapwood
is thin and pale brown. Both wood and bark have a
distinct odor of tannic acid.

Uses. Scrub oak is used for rough construction,
farm repairs, fencing, fuel, and mine timbers. Because
of the inaccessibility and poor form of the tree, the wood
is not of commercial value; it is of local value only.

PACIFIC POST OAK OR WHITE OAK

(*Quercus garryana*)

The Pacific post oak is found commonly throughout the Pacific Coast region from Canada southward to southern California, occurring at various elevations from sea level to 4000 feet. It reaches its best development in western Washington, where it attains a height of 60 to 90 feet and a diameter of 1 to 3 feet.

Form. The stem is straight, cylindrical, and clear of branches for one fourth to one third the total height; the crown is broad, spreading, rounded, and composed of large, more or less upright, branches. At higher elevations the growth is shrubby. The root system is deep and spreading.

Occurrence. The Pacific post oak thrives best in the deep, moist, fertile, open soils of river bottoms and high valleys, usually occurring in open pure stands. Frequently it is found in mixture with Douglas fir, madroña, ash, and yellow pine.

Distinctive characteristics. The Pacific post oak may be distinguished by (1) the deeply lobed (frequently notched), smooth-margined, thick, shiny, deep-green leaves; (2) the oblong, full, rounded acorns, set in the shallow, scaly cups; (3) the grayish, hairy twigs, with large, full, pointed, hairy winter buds; and (4) the light grayish-brown, scaly bark of old stems, broken into broad ridges by deep fissures.

Wood. The wood is heavy, hard, strong, rather tough, of uniform texture, and durable; it seasons fairly well, is rather difficult to work, but takes a fine finish. The heartwood is a pale yellowish brown; the sapwood is thin and nearly white.

Uses.   Pacific post oak is used for agricultural imple-

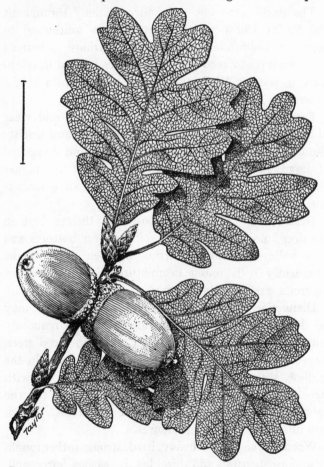

Fig. 67.   The lobed and notched leaf, and the large, full acorn of the Pacific post oak.

ments, wagon stock, tight cooperage, shipbuilding, interior finishing, cabinetwork, fencing, and fuel. It is the principal timber oak of the western United States.

The Pacific post oak is of attractive appearance and is much used as an ornamental tree for shade purposes about farm buildings or in the pasture. Occasionally it is used in park and other large plantings.

CALIFORNIA WHITE OAK OR VALLEY OAK
(*Quercus lobata*)

The California white oak is distributed throughout that portion of California west of the Sierra Nevada Mountains, occurring at various elevations from sea level to 5000 feet. It reaches its best development in the Sacramento Valley, where it attains a height of 60 to 100 feet and a diameter of 2 to 4 feet.

Form. The crown is broad, full, spreading, and composed of large branches which join the stem at right angles; the stem is short, straight, thick, and clear of branches for about one fourth the total height. The drooping character of the small branches and twigs gives the tree a " weeping " appearance. The root system is deep and spreading.

Occurrence. The California white oak thrives best in the deep, moist, open, fertile soils of river bottoms, where it forms extensive park-like stands. It occupies low plateaus where the surface is dry but the level of ground water lies at no great depth.

Distinctive characteristics. The California white oak may be distinguished by (1) the oblong, deeply lobed, smooth-margined, dark-green (undersides pale green) leaves; (2) the long ($1\frac{1}{2}$ to 2 inches), conical, chestnut-brown, edible acorns, set one fourth in the hairy cups,

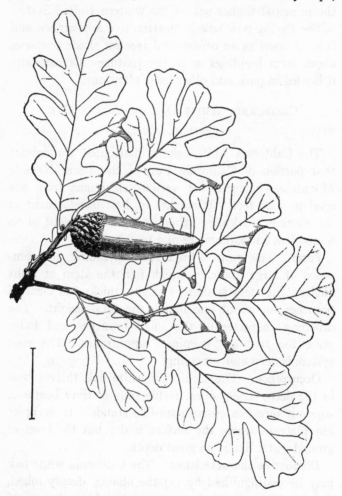

Fig. 68. The deeply lobed leaf and the long, conical acorn of the California white oak.

which are covered with thick scales; (3) the fine, ashy-gray twigs; (4) the thick, grayish bark of old stems, broken into broad, flat ridges by deep fissures; and (5) the " weeping " form.

Wood. The wood is heavy, hard, rather brittle, frequently cross-grained, and durable; it seasons fairly well, is difficult to work, but takes a fair finish. The heartwood is a light brown; the sapwood is thick and pale brown.

Uses. Because of its poor form and the heavy demand for fuel wood, the California white oak is utilized almost entirely for this purpose. Occasionally it is sawed for rough construction, farm repairs, and fencing.

The California white oak is a very attractive ornamental tree, and scattered specimens should be retained about the farm buildings and in the pastures for shade purposes. The acorns (mast) are of considerable value as feed. Occasionally the California white oak is used in park and cemetery plantings.

Rock Oak or Blue Oak

(Quercus douglasii)

The rock oak (or blue oak, so called because of its vivid blue-green foliage) is found commonly throughout that portion of California west of the Sierra Nevada Mountains, occurring at various elevations from sea level to 4000 feet. It reaches its best development in northern California, where it attains a height of 40 to 80 feet and a diameter of 2 to 4 feet.

Form. The stem is more or less crooked and clear of branches for about one third the total height; the crown is compact, dome-like, symmetrical, and composed of spreading, upright branches.   At higher elevations the growth is shrubby.   The root system is deep and spreading.

Fig. 69.   The small, almost entire leaf, and the comparatively large, oblong acorn of the rock oak.

Occurrence.   The rock oak thrives best in the deep, moist, open soils of the foothill valleys and lower slopes, where it forms extensive open stands with the other oaks and pines.   It often occurs in dry situations where the soil is open and sandy and the level of ground water is at no great depth.

Distinctive characteristics.   The rock oak may be distinguished by (1) the blue-green foliage; (2) the entire (or sparsely toothed or bristle-pointed), hairy leaves, which are blue-green above and yellow-green below; (3) the fine, hairy, grayish-brown twigs; (4) the thin, pale grayish-brown, soft, scaly bark of old stems, broken into narrow ridges by shallow fissures; (5) the oblong (or conical), pointed, chestnut-brown acorns, about an inch long, set in shallow, scaly cups; and (6) the rounded, symmetrical crown.

Wood. The wood is heavy, hard, strong, stiff, brittle, dense, tough, cross-grained, but not durable; it seasons badly, is difficult to work, but takes a fine finish. The heartwood is dark brown; the sapwood is thick and pale brown.

Uses. Because of the poor form and small amount of usable material, the rock oak is seldom manufactured for industrial use. The wood possesses a high fuel value, and it is for this purpose mostly that the tree is utilized. Large stems are frequently defective because of heart rot.

The rock oak has an attractive appearance, but it is seldom used as an ornamental tree because of the slow growth. Where it occurs naturally, scattered specimens are retained for shade purposes.

CALIFORNIA BLACK OAK
(*Quercus californica*)

The California black oak has a general distribution throughout the Pacific Coast region from Oregon southward to the Mexican border, occurring at elevations of 1500 to 3000 feet in the northern part of its range and from 4000 to 8000 feet in the southern part. It reaches its best development in northern California, where it attains a height of 80 to 100 feet and a diameter of 2 to 4 feet.

Form. The stem is short, more or less crooked, and clear of branches for about one fourth the total height; the crown is spreading, irregularly rounded, and composed of stout branches. Frequently the growth is shrubby. The root system is deep and spreading.

Occurrence. The California black oak thrives best in the deep, moist, open soils of cañon bottoms and upper mountain slopes, where it occurs in a pure stand or in mixture with Douglas fir, yellow pine, incense cedar, laurel, and the oaks.

Distinctive characteristics. The California black oak may be distinguished by (1) the firm, oblong, deeply lobed, bristle-pointed, glossy, yellow-green leaves, the undersides of which are pale green and more or less hairy; (2) the oblong, indistinctly striped, more or less hairy, light reddish-brown acorns, set one half to two thirds in the stalked, thickened, scaly, yellow-brown cups; (3) the smooth, grayish-brown bark of young stems and branches; (4) the thick, hard, grayish brown-black bark of old stems, broken into broad ridges and oblong plates by shallow fissures; and (5) the irregular form.

Wood. The tree is moderately heavy, hard, not strong, brittle, coarse-grained, and not durable; it seasons well, is easily worked, and takes a fair finish. The heartwood is a light reddish-brown; the sapwood is pale red. The tree is susceptible to heart rot.

Uses. California black oak is used for rough construction, farm repair material, and fuel. It is of little commercial value because of the poor form and inferior quality of the wood.

The California black oak is occasionally used for ornamental purposes but is not so satisfactory as the other

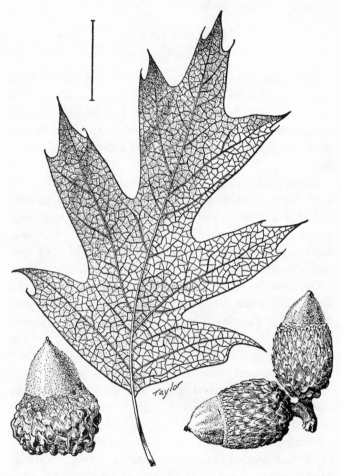

FIG. 70.   California black oak. Note the sharp, bristle-pointed lobes of the
leaf, and the heavy, thickened acorn cups.

trees which thrive in the same situation. In the sapling stage it presents a pleasing contrast in a group planting of darker-foliaged trees.

Highland Live Oak
(*Quercus wislizeni*)

The highland live oak is distributed throughout the mountains of California at elevations of 1500 to 7000 feet. It reaches its best development in the mountain valleys of central California, where it attains a height of 60 to 80 feet and a diameter of 2 to 6 feet.

Form. The stem is short, straight, and clear of branches for one fourth to one third the total height; the crown is moderately spreading, rounded, and composed of thick, rather ascending branches. At lower elevations the growth is quite shrubby. The root system is deep and spreading.

Occurrence. The highland live oak thrives best in the deep, moist, open, fertile soils of sheltered cañon bottoms, where it is associated with other oaks, the mountain birch, and the sycamore. Occasionally it occurs in the sandy or stony soil of dry washes, but the growth is poor. It is rarely found in a pure stand.

Distinctive characteristics. The highland live oak may be distinguished by (1) the small, oval, spiny-toothed or entire, leathery, glossy, flat, deep-green leaves, the undersides of which are yellow-green, and the short, hairy leaf stems; (2) the oblong, pointed, chestnut-brown acorns, set one third to one half in the deep, scaly, hairy, light-brown cups; (3) the thick, dark-brown bark of old stems, broken into broad, rounded, connected ridges by shallow fissures; and (4) the open, irregular crown.

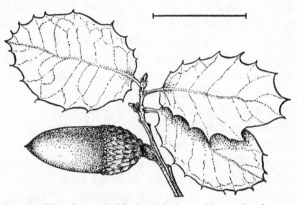

FIG. 71. The spiny-toothed leaf and the large, oblong, pointed acorn of the highland live oak.

Wood. The wood is heavy, hard, strong, dense, tough, close-grained, and moderately durable; it seasons poorly, is difficult to work, but takes a fine finish. The heartwood is a light reddish brown; the sapwood is thick and nearly white.

Uses. Highland live oak is used for rough construction, farm repairs, tool handles, wagon stock, fencing, and fuel. Because of its limited supply and its inaccessibility, the highland live oak is not manufactured commercially. It is of considerable value locally, however.

The highland live oak is a beautiful ornamental tree in its sapling and pole stages and is occasionally planted about ranch buildings.

CAÑON LIVE OAK OR MAUL OAK

(*Quercus chrysolepis*)

The cañon live oak is distributed throughout the Pacific Slope from southern Oregon southward to Lower California, and inland along the mountains of southern Arizona and New Mexico. In the northern part of its range it is found at various elevations from sea level to 2500 feet, and in the southern part at elevations of 3000 to 9000 feet. It reaches its best development in the sheltered cañon bottoms of central California, where it attains a height of 30 to 50 feet and a diameter of 3 to 5 feet.

Form. The stem is short, thick, and clear of branches for about one fourth to one third the total height; the crown is dense, rounded, and spreading, the large, horizontal branches extending outward from the stem for a distance of 50 to 75 feet. The root system is deep and spreading.

Occurrence. The cañon live oak thrives best in the deep, moist, fertile, open soils of cañon bottoms, where it occurs in small pure clumps or in mixture with other oaks, yellow pine, and incense cedar. In dry situations the growth is shrubby.

Distinctive characteristics. The cañon live oak may be distinguished by (1) the persistent, oblong, thick, pronouncedly toothed or nearly entire, yellow-green leaves, the lower sides of which are first covered with yellow hairs and later are smooth and of a blue-green color; (2) the oblong, chestnut-brown acorns, 1 to 2 inches long, set in shallow, scaly cups, which are densely covered with pale-yellow hairs; (3) the thick, soft,

scaly, grayish-brown bark, broken into narrow ridges
by shallow fissures; and (4) the spreading form.

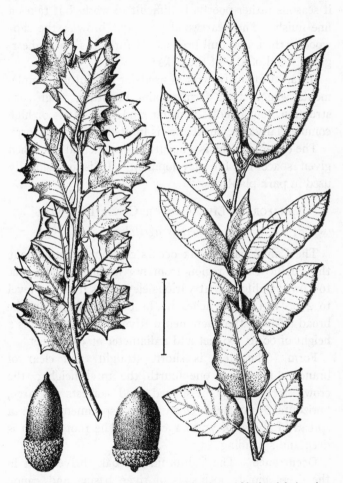

FIG. 72. Cañon live oak, showing the varying forms of leaf and fruit. As a
rule the larger the tree, the less spiny the leaf.

Wood. The wood is heavy, hard, strong, tough, stiff, of uniform texture, usually fine-grained, and durable; it seasons rather poorly, is difficult to work, but takes a fine finish. The heartwood is a light brown; the sapwood is thick and dull brown. It furnishes the highest-grade wood of any of the oaks.

Uses. Cañon live oak is used for agricultural implements, wagon stock, farm repairs, furniture, rough construction, tool handles, fencing, and fuel. It is of high commercial value, but its use is limited by its poor form.

The cañon live oak is a beautiful ornamental tree when given space for full development. It is occasionally used in park plantings.

CALIFORNIA LIVE OAK OR COAST LIVE OAK
(*Quercus agrifolia*)

The California live oak occurs commonly throughout the Pacific Coast region from north-central California to Lower California, at various elevations from sea level to 4000 feet. It reaches its best development in the broad basin of the Sacramento River, where it attains a height of 60 to 100 feet and a diameter of 3 to 6 feet.

Form. The stem is short, straight, and clear of branches for about one fourth the total height; the crown is broad, dome-shaped, and consists of large, horizontal branches. Open-grown specimens have a spread of crown of 75 to 150 feet. The root system is deep and spreading.

Occurrence. The California live oak thrives best in the deep, moist, open soils of river basins and cañon bottoms, where it occurs in a pure stand or in mixture with the oaks, sycamore, alder, and spruce.   In exposed situations and at higher elevations the growth is shrubby.

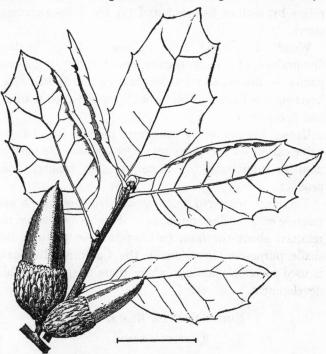

Fig. 73.   The bristle-pointed leaf and conical, pointed acorn of the California live oak.   Note the deep cups and the coarse cup scales.

Distinctive characteristics. The California live oak may be distinguished by (1) the bristle-toothed (or entire), firm, oval, dark-green leaves, the edges of which are incurving and the undersides a pale-green color and covered with short hairs; (2) the conical, pointed, light chestnut-brown acorns, set about one third in the incurving scaly cups; (3) the smooth, pale grayish bark of young stems and branches; (4) the thick, hard, dark-brown bark of old stems, broken into broad, rounded ridges by shallow fissures; and (5) the wide-spreading crown.

Wood. The wood is heavy, hard, strong, brittle, fine-grained, of uniform texture, and durable; it seasons poorly, is difficult to work, but takes a fine finish. The heartwood is light reddish brown; the sapwood is thick and dull brown.

Uses. Because of its poor form the wood is of little value except for fuel purposes. Occasionally the bark is used to adulterate the more valuable tanbark oak product.

The huge, scattered, open-grown trees present an attractive orchard-like appearance. Single trees should be retained about the farm buildings and in pastures for shade purposes. Occasionally the California live oak is used in large plantings where there is space for full development.

EMORY OAK OR BLACK OAK

(*Quercus emoryi*)

The Emory oak is distributed throughout the arid southwestern United States from Texas westward to California and southward into Mexico, occurring at elevations of 5000 to 10,000 feet. It reaches its best development in the sheltered cañons of the mountains of Arizona and New Mexico, where it attains a height of 50 to 75 feet and a diameter of 2 to 4 feet.

Form. The stem is short, straight, and clear of branches for one fourth to one third the total height;

the crown is open, spreading, rounded, and composed of large, rigid, horizontal branches. In the open the crown

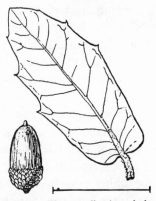

FIG. 74. The small, irregularly toothed leaf, and the small, oblong acorn of the Emory oak.

occasionally has a spread of 75 to 100 feet. In exposed situations the growth is shrubby. The root system is deep and spreading.

Occurrence. The Emory oak thrives best in the deep, moist, open soils of sheltered cañon bottoms and protected mesas, where it occurs in mixture with the piñon pines, Jeffrey pine, Douglas fir, and the cañon hardwoods. Occasionally it occurs in a pure stand.

Distinctive characteristics. The Emory oak may be distinguished by (1) the small, oblong, lance-pointed, entire or irregularly toothed, rigid, glossy, dark-green leaves, the undersides of which are a paler green and more or less hairy; (2) the small, oblong, pointed, dark chestnut-brown, sweet acorns, set one third to one half in the deep, hairy, scaly, pale-brown cups; (3) the hairy, red twigs, becoming smooth and dark red-brown; and (4) the thick, hard, brown-black bark of old stems, broken into large, oblong, thick plates by shallow fissures.

Wood. The wood is heavy, hard, strong, rather brittle, close-grained, but not durable; it seasons fairly well, is difficult to work, but takes a fine finish. The heartwood is dark brown; the sapwood is thick and vivid brown.

Uses. Emory oak is used locally for rough construction, farm repairs, fencing, tool handles, furniture, and fuel. The utilization of this tree is limited by its inaccessibility and poor form. It has a relatively important place among timber trees because of the dearth of other good timber in the hardwood forests of this region.

The Emory oak is an attractive ornamental tree and is occasionally planted for yard and street purposes.

Tanbark Oak

(*Quercus densiflora* or *Pasania densiflora*)

The tanbark oak is distributed throughout that part of the Pacific Coast region west of the Sierra Nevada Mountains from southern Oregon to southern California, occurring at elevations of a few hundred feet to 4000 feet. It reaches its best development in the coast ranges of northern California, where it attains a height of 80 to 100 feet and a diameter of 2 to 6 feet.

Form. The stem is long, straight, and clear of branches for one half to two thirds the total height; the crown is narrow and rather flat. In the open the crown is spreading and full and the stem is short and thick. The root system is deep and spreading.

Occurrence. The tanbark oak thrives best in the deep, moist, open, sandy soils of river and cañon bottoms,

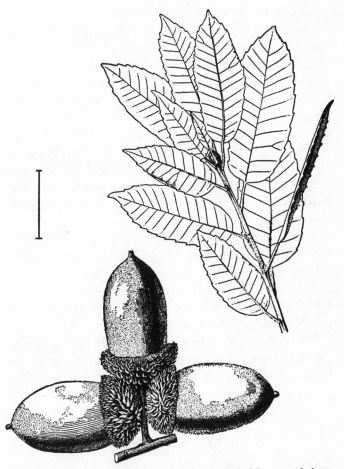

FIG. 75. Tanbark oak. Branch showing sharply toothed leaves, and cluster of large acorns. Note the curved, outstanding cup scales.

where it is associated with redwood, Douglas fir, and other hardwoods. Occasionally it forms rather extensive pure stands.

Distinctive characteristics. The tanbark oak may be distinguished by (1) the medium-sized, sharply toothed, oblong, persistent, light-green leaves, which are covered with rusty hairs on the undersides; (2) the large, oblong acorns, set in shallow cups, covered with pointed, curved scales; (3) the thick, smooth, grayish-brown bark, broken into broad plates by narrow fissures (see Figure 12); and (4) the woolly appearance of new twigs.

Wood. The wood is heavy, hard, strong, very dense, of uniform texture, rather brittle, and durable; it seasons well, is difficult to work, but takes a fine finish. The heartwood is a light reddish-brown; the sapwood is thin and brown.

Uses. Tanbark oak is used for general construction, agricultural implements, wagon stock, interior finishing, flooring, furniture, fencing, farm repairs, and fuel.

The bark is extensively used in the production of tannic acid for the tanning of leather, and it is from this use that the tree gets its name.

The open-grown tanbark oak, with its spreading crown of huge branches and the dense foliage, is an extremely attractive ornamental tree for yard or park purposes. A few trees in a pasture furnish the shade needed by stock in a warm climate.

The Sycamores (*Platanus*)

The two Western sycamores resemble each other rather closely, but as they occur in widely separated regions there should be but little confusion in distinguishing them.

ARIZONA SYCAMORE

(*Platanus wrightii*)

The Arizona sycamore has a general distribution throughout the southern part of New Mexico and Arizona and southward into Mexico, occurring at elevations of 4000 to 6000 feet. In favorable situations it attains a height of 60 to 80 feet and a diameter of 3 to 5 feet.

Form. The stem is straight, cylindrical, and clear of branches for one fourth to one half the total height; the crown is open, spreading, rounded, and composed of large ascending branches. The root system is deep and spreading.

Occurrence. The sycamore thrives best in the deep, moist, open, fertile soils of cañon bottoms and mountain valleys, where it is associated with cottonwood, birch, and the willows. It never occurs in a pure stand.

Distinctive characteristics. The Arizona sycamore may be distinguished by (1) the large, irregularly toothed, star-shaped, glossy, light-green leaves; (2) the leaf stem, which completely incloses the bud at its base; (3) the fruit balls, which hang in groups of several on a stem, the stem passing through each ball; (4) the

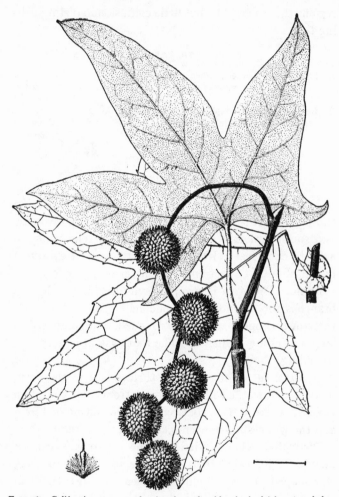

Fig. 76. California sycamore, showing the under side of a leaf (above) and the upper side (below). Note the manner in which the stem of the fruit cluster passes through each "buttonball." Note also the prominent stipule at the right, and the tufted seed in the lower left-hand corner.

moderately coarse, zigzag, ashy-brown twigs; (5) the
thin, smooth, creamy bark of small stems and branches;
and (6) the thick, dark-brown bark of old stems, broken
into broad, rounded, scaly ridges by deep fissures.

Wood. The wood is heavy, hard, moderately strong,
tough, but not durable; it seasons badly, is difficult to
work, but takes a fine finish. The heartwood is a light
reddish brown; the sapwood is thick and pale brown.
The quarter-sawed wood shows a very pleasing grain.

Uses. Arizona sycamore is used for rough construction, interior finishing, tobacco boxes, mine timbers,
fuel, and farm repairs. It is the largest and most valuable hardwood tree of the region.

The Arizona sycamore is an attractive ornamental
tree and is much used for street and yard plantings. If
the young trees are irrigated until established they will
maintain themselves in dry situations, provided the soil
is deep and open.

CALIFORNIA SYCAMORE OR BUTTONBALL
(*Platanus racemosa*)

The California sycamore is distributed throughout
that part of California which extends from about the
central portion of the state to the Mexican border, occurring at various elevations from sea level to 5000 feet.
Under favorable conditions it attains a height of 50 to
80 feet and a diameter of 2 to 6 feet.

Form. The stem is long, straight, cylindrical, and
clear of branches for one third to one half the total
height of the tree; the crown is open, irregularly rounded,
and composed of large, crooked, spreading branches.

In the open the stem usually splits up into several large branches at a height of 8 or 10 feet above ground. The root system is spreading.

Occurrence. The California sycamore thrives best in the deep, moist, open soils of stream bottoms and gulches, where it is associated with alder, maple, the willows, and walnut. It never occurs in a pure stand.

Distinctive characteristics. The California sycamore may be distinguished by (1) the large, more or less toothed, three- to five-lobed, firm, yellow-green leaves, the undersides of which are a paler green and more or less hairy; (2) the leaf stem, which completely inclosed the bud at its base; (3) the fruit balls, which hang in groups of several on a stem, the stem passing through each ball; (4) the thin, reddish-brown bark of young stems and small branches; (5) the thick, scaly, dark-brown bark of old stems, broken into broad, rounded ridges by deep fissures; and (6) the open, spreading crown.

Wood. The wood is heavy, hard, strong, tough, difficult to split, of uniform texture, close-grained, rather brittle, but not durable; it seasons badly, is difficult to work, but takes a fine finish. The heartwood is a pale reddish brown; the sapwood is thick and pale brown.

Uses. California sycamore is used for interior finishing, pulley blocks, farm repairs, and rough construction. The demand is limited by the small supply.

The California sycamore forms a striking ornamental tree and is extensively planted throughout the western United States. As a street tree it presents a fine, graceful appearance.

SECTION 3. TREES WITH SIMPLE LEAVES

A. LEAVES WITH TOOTHED MARGIN

BLACK BIRCH	CHINQUAPIN
ALDERS	POPLARS
CHERRIES	BLACK WILLOW
PALO BLANCO	

Black Birch

(*Betula occidentalis*)

The black birch is distributed throughout the Rocky Mountains from Canada southward to northern New Mexico and from Puget Sound eastward to the Black Hills of South Dakota. In the southern part of its range it occurs at elevations of 3000 to 8000 feet. It reaches its best development in Washington and Idaho, where it attains a height of 80 to 120 feet and a diameter of 2 to 4 feet.

Form. The stem is long, straight, and clear of branches for about one third the total height; the crown is compact, open, broadly rounded, and composed of numerous small, upright branches with drooping twigs, giving the tree a " weeping " aspect. The root system is deep and spreading.

Occurrence. The black birch thrives best in the deep, moist, open, fertile, sandy or gravelly soils of river and cañon bottoms, where it is associated with the willows, maple, sycamore, and the firs. It never occurs in a pure stand.

Distinctive characteristics. The black birch may be distinguished by (1) the thin, orange-brown bark, peel-

FIG. 77. Fruiting twig of the black birch. The cones or catkins contain hundreds of small seeds, each one with its overlapping scale. Individual seeds and a scale are shown in the lower left-hand corner. The seed at the extreme left is enlarged to twice natural size:

ing in " papery " sheets to display the orange inner bark; (2) the orange-brown twigs, covered with hairs when they first appear; (3) the broadly oval, doubly toothed leaves, which are dull green above and yellow-green below; and (4) the erect, brown cones, about $1\frac{1}{2}$ inches long and $\frac{1}{3}$ inch in diameter.

Wood. The wood is heavy, hard, strong, of uniform texture, close-grained, but not durable; it seasons badly, is rather difficult to work, but takes a fine finish. The heartwood is pale brown; the sapwood is thick and nearly white.

Uses. Black birch is used for rough construction, wagon stock, cooperage, furniture, and fuel. Where it occurs in quantity it is of considerable commercial value and is in demand in many industries.

The black birch is a valuable ornamental tree and deserves a much wider utilization than it has at present. The form is extremely graceful and attractive, and the contrast of the green foliage and the light bark is most striking. The young tree has a dense, pyramidal crown and is suited to yard plantings.

The Alders (*Alnus*)

KEY TO THE ALDERS

A. Bark ashy gray, smooth . . . . . RED ALDER (*A. oregona*)
B. Bark dull brown, scaly . . . WHITE ALDER (*A. rhombifolia*)

RED ALDER

(*Alnus oregona*)

The red alder has a general distribution over the Pacific states from Canada southward to a point near the Mexican border, occurring at elevations of a few hundred feet to 5000 feet. It reaches its best development in the Puget Sound region, where it attains a height of 80 to 100 feet and a diameter of 2 to 4 feet.

Form. The stem is straight, long, cylindrical, and clear of branches for one half to two thirds the total height; the crown is rather open, broadly dome-like, and composed of numerous small branches which droop at the ends. The root system is deep and spreading.

Occurrence. The red alder thrives best in the deep, moist, open soils of river bottoms, where it is associated with the firs, the willows, maple, and spruce. In the mountains it occupies the cañon bottoms. It rarely occurs in a pure stand.

Distinctive characteristics. The red alder may be distinguished by (1) the large, oblong, doubly toothed, deep yellow-green leaves, covered with hairs; (2) the thin, smooth, light ashy-gray bark of old stems (Figure 9); (3) the shiny, red-brown, glossy winter twigs; (4) the persistent woody cones, about 1 inch long; and (5) the dark-red, stalked, scurfy winter buds, about $\frac{1}{3}$ inch long.

Wood. The wood is light, weak, moderately hard, brittle, of even texture, close-grained, but not durable; it seasons rather badly, but works easily and takes a fair finish. The heartwood is a light brown, tinged with red; the sapwood is thick and nearly white. Upon exposure to the air the sapwood turns a brilliant red, hence the name.

Uses. Red alder is used for furniture, interior finishing, general construction, sashes and doors, wagon stock, treatment posts, cooperage, woodenware, and fuel.

Where it occurs in quantities, the red alder is considered to possess great commercial value.

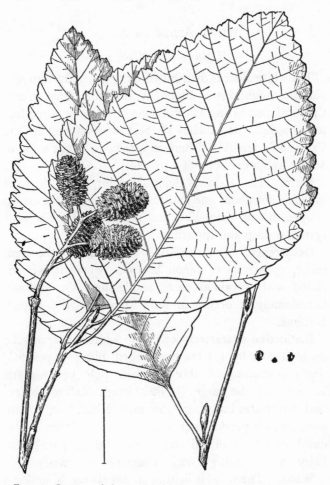

FIG. 78. Leaves and cluster of fruiting cones of the red alder. Note the stalked character of the buds.

The red alder possesses a graceful and beautiful form and is much used in ornamental plantings.

WHITE ALDER OR ALDER

(*Alnus rhombifolia*)

The white alder is distributed quite generally throughout the mountains of Idaho, Washington, Oregon, and California, occurring at elevations of a few hundred feet to 4000 feet. It reaches its best development in the Cascade Mountains, where it attains a height of 60 to 80 feet and a diameter of 2 to 4 feet.

Form. The stem is long, straight, and clear of branches for about one half the total height; the crown is open, broad, dome-like, and symmetrical. The root system is deep and spreading.

Occurrence. The white alder thrives best in the deep, moist, open soils of cañon bottoms, where it is associated with sycamore, ash, maple, and the willows. Occasionally it occurs in pure stands in the stream bottoms.

Distinctive characteristics. The white alder may be distinguished by (1) the egg-shaped, blunt or pointed, singly (sometimes doubly) toothed, pale yellow-green leaves; (2) the large ($\frac{1}{2}$ inch long), stalked, hairy, dark-red winter buds; (3) the small ($\frac{1}{2}$ inch long) woody cones, which persist over winter; (4) the thin, scaly, dull-brown bark of old stems; and (5) the pale-green, hairy twigs, turning a dark orange-red and glossy.

Wood. The wood is light, soft, not strong, of uniform texture, close-grained, brittle, and not durable; it seasons rather badly, but works easily and takes a fine finish. The heartwood is a pale yellowish brown; the sapwood is thick and nearly white.

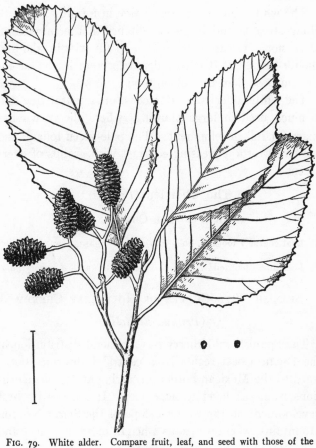

FIG. 79. White alder. Compare fruit, leaf, and seed with those of the red alder (Fig. 78).

Uses. White alder is used for rough construction, interior finishing, wagon stock, cooperage, woodenware, boxes and crates, cabinetwork, sashes and doors, and fuel. It is marketed with red alder under the trade name of " alder."

The white alder is of great value in forming a growth along streams and irrigation ditches in the prevention of erosion. Occasionally it is used for windbreaks and shelter belts, but it is considered to be of less value for this purpose than the cottonwoods.

The white alder is an attractive ornamental tree and is much used in large plantings where the crown has space for full development. The pale-green foliage and red twigs form a pleasing contrast with groups of evergreens.

The Cherries (*Prunus*)

KEY TO THE CHERRIES

A. Leaf coarsely toothed, holly-like . . SPANISH WILD CHERRY
(*P. ilicifolia*)
B. Leaf finely toothed . . . . BITTER CHERRY (*P. emarginata*)

SPANISH WILD CHERRY OR HOLLYLEAF CHERRY

(*Prunus ilicifolia*)

The Spanish wild cherry has a general distribution in the Pacific Coast region from central California southward to the Mexican border, occurring at various elevations from sea level to 4000 feet. It reaches its best development on the western slope of the Sierra Nevada Mountains, where it attains a height of 20 to 30 feet and a diameter of 1 to 2 feet.

Form. The stem is rather short, straight, and clear of branches for about one fourth the total height; the crown is dense, compact, oblong, and composed of small ascending branches. Frequently the growth is very shrubby. The root system is spreading.

Occurrence. The Spanish wild cherry thrives best in the deep, moist, open, sandy soils of the stream bottoms and lower foothill slopes, where it is associated with the chaparral trees. At higher elevations it forms a dense shrubby growth.

Distinctive characteristics. The Spanish wild cherry may be distinguished by (1) the small, oval, spiny-toothed, thick, persistent, dark-green, shiny leaves; (2) the bitter taste of the twigs; (3) the clusters of large ($\frac{1}{2}$ to $\frac{2}{3}$ inch), red to nearly black, tart, palatable fruits; (4) the smooth, orange to red-brown twigs; (5) the deep, red-brown bark of old stems, broken into plate-like ridges by shallow fissures; and (6) the dense, oblong crown of dark-green foliage.

Wood. The wood is heavy, hard, dense, tough, strong, fine-grained, of uniform texture, but not durable; it seasons poorly, but is moderately easy to work and takes a fine finish. The heartwood is a light red-brown; the sapwood is thick and pale brown.

Uses. Spanish wild cherry is used for fuel, novelties, farm repairs, treatment post material, and wood turning. Its use is limited by the small supply.

The Spanish wild cherry is occasionally planted in the United States and Europe for ornamental purposes, for which it is well suited. Because of its narrow crown it is adapted to plantings in yards and on narrow streets.

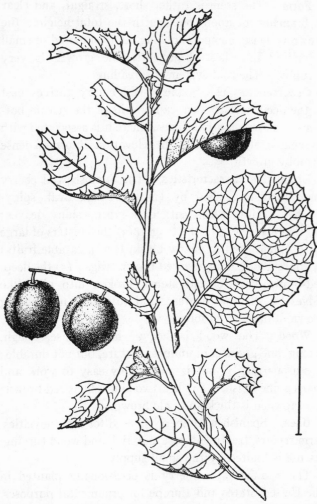

FIG. 80. Branch of Spanish cherry, showing the spiny-toothed leaf and the smooth, round fruit.

Occasionally it is used for shelter-belt purposes about the orchard.

Bitter Cherry or Wild Plum

(*Prunus emarginata*)

The bitter cherry is distributed throughout the Rocky Mountain system from Canada southward to a point near the Mexican border, occurring at various elevations from sea level to 3000 feet in the northern part of its range and from 5000 to 9000 feet in the southern part. It reaches its best development in western Washington, where it attains a height of 30 to 40 feet and a diameter of 12 to 15 inches.

Form. The stem of the forest-grown tree is long, straight, and clear of branches for one third to one half the total height; the crown is open, oblong, symmetrical, and composed of small ascending branches. Frequently the growth is shrubby. The root system is spreading.

Occurrence. The bitter cherry thrives best in the deep, moist, open, fertile soils of the stream bottoms, where it is associated with Douglas fir, maple, sycamore, and the willows. Occasionally it forms rather extensive pure stands.

Distinctive characteristics. The bitter cherry may be distinguished by (1) the finely toothed, oblong, firm, glossy, persistent, dark-green leaves; (2) the characteristically bitter taste of the twigs; (3) the clusters of red to nearly black, bitter fruits; (4) the thin, smooth, dark-brown bark of old stems, marked by orange lenticels; (5) the reddish-brown bark of twigs; and (6) the open, graceful form.

Wood. The wood is light, weak, brittle, moderately hard, but not durable; it seasons poorly, but works easily and takes a fair finish. The heartwood is light

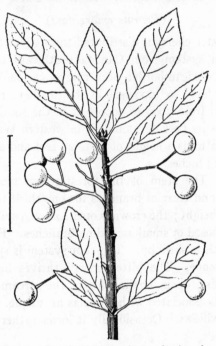

Fig. 81. Branch of bitter cherry, showing the narrow, oblong leaves, and the clusters of small round fruit.

brown, frequently mottled; the sapwood is thick and nearly white.

Uses. Bitter cherry is used for fuel, treatment posts, farm repairs, and rough construction. It is seldom of sufficient size to warrant commercial manufacture.

Along with its associated trees, the bitter cherry possesses considerable value in the holding of stream banks and the prevention of erosion. Planted about the orchard, it affords protection from bird damage, as the birds prefer the wild fruits to the cultivated fruits.

Chinquapin

(*Castanopsis chrysophylla*)

The chinquapin occurs commonly throughout the Sierra Nevada and coast range mountains from Canada southward to the Mexican border at elevations of 2000 to 10,000 feet. It reaches its best development in the humid coast valleys of northern California, where it attains a height of 100 to 150 feet and a diameter of 4 to 10 feet.

Form. The stem is long, straight, cylindrical, and clear of branches for one half to two thirds the total height; the crown is compact, broadly dome-shaped, and composed of stout, spreading branches and stiff branchlets. The root system is deep and spreading.

Occurrence. The chinquapin thrives best in the deep, moist, open soils of the humid river valleys of the northern Pacific Coast, where it is associated with redwood, Douglas fir, and the other hardwoods. At high elevations there occurs a shrubby form, which develops a dense ground cover below the Jeffrey pine, Western juniper, and white fir.

Distinctive characteristics. The chinquapin may be distinguished by (1) the purple-red, edible, chestnut-like seed, only partly inclosed by the spiny bur; (2) the thick, oblong, pointed, persistent, yellow-green leaves, the edges of which curl toward the lower side, which

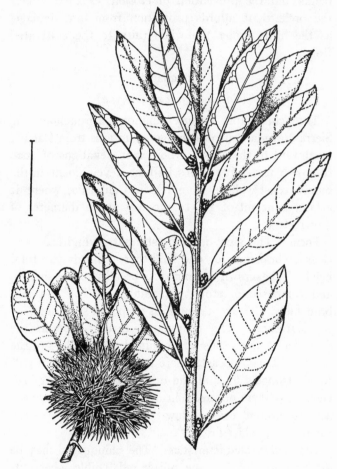

FIG. 82.   Chinquapin, showing the chestnut-like bur and portion of seed, and the stiff, oblong leaves.

is covered with a thick coating of golden-yellow hairs; (3) the stiff, reddish-brown twigs, covered at first with golden hairs, and later smooth; and (4) the thick brownish bark, broken into broad ridges by deep fissures.

Wood. The wood is rather soft, light, moderately strong, brittle, of uniform texture, and durable; it seasons well, works easily, and takes a fine finish. The heartwood is a pale reddish brown; the sapwood is thin and nearly white. The wood resembles that of the chestnut.

Uses. Chinquapin is used for agricultural implements, wagon stock, rough construction, interior finishing, shingles, fence posts, crossties, and flooring.

At high elevations the shrubby growth of chinquapin, together with mountain lilac and manzanita, constitutes an important factor in watershed protection and flood prevention.

The chinquapin is occasionally used ornamentally; it presents a very pleasing contrast when seen against any of the darker-foliaged evergreens.

The Poplars (*Populus*)

KEY TO THE POPLARS

A. Leaf round or nearly round, finely
   toothed . . . . ASPEN (*P. tremuloides*)
B. Leaf ovate or heart-shaped, coarsely toothed
   1. LEAF STEM ROUND; BARK ASHY
      GRAY . . . . BLACK COTTONWOOD
                                        (*P. trichocarpa*)
   2. LEAF STEM FLAT; BARK DARK
      BROWN . . . . WHITE COTTONWOOD
                                        (*P. fremontii*)

Aspen

(Populus tremuloides)

The aspen is distributed very generally throughout the northern part of the United States. In the West it is found mostly in the Rocky Mountains, extending from Canada to Northern Arizona, New Mexico, and Central California. It is a characteristic tree of moist mountain meadows and seeps. Under favorable conditions it attains a height of 40 to 80 feet and a diameter of 1 to 2 feet.

Form. The stem is straight, cylindrical, moderately long, and clear of branches; the crown is very open, rounded, and composed of numerous upright branches.

Occurrence. The aspen is a common tree on " burns " and cut-over areas, where it serves as a " nurse " tree to the more tolerant pines. The slowly melting snows of the Northern states leave the soil in a moist condition, very favorable to the germination of the cottony, wind-blown seeds. Because of its intolerance (of shade) it is unable to compete with the trees which occupy the better situations, except when openings are made in such places by fire or logging.

Distinctive characteristics. The aspen may be distinguished by (1) the finely toothed, glossy, bright-green, almost round leaves; (2) the " trembling " of the leaves; (3) the flattened leaf stems; (4) the open rounded crown; (5) the smooth, grayish-green bark of twigs and young stems; (6) the dark, broken bark of old trees; and (7) the thickets of " suckers " which spring from the roots.

Wood. The wood of the aspen is light, soft, brittle, dents without splitting, and is not durable; it seasons

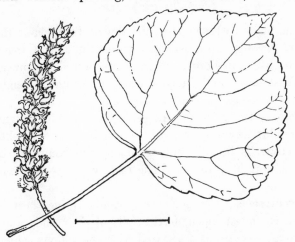

FIG. 83. Fruiting catkin and the leaf of the aspen. Compare with the other poplars.

well, works easily, and takes a fair finish. The heartwood is nearly white; the sapwood is similar in color.

Uses. Aspen is used extensively in the manufacture of wood pulp and excelsior. It is also used for slack cooperage, wood turning, treatment posts, rough construction, woodenware, and wagon boxes. It is sold under the trade name of "poplar."

Aspen is an important tree in the natural reforestation of burned areas and as a " nurse " cover for the more valuable pines and spruces. As an ornamental tree it possesses some value for quick-effect group plantings in natural landscaping. The " trembling " character of the foliage affords a pleasing contrast to the more stately hardwoods and evergreens.

Black Cottonwood

(*Populus trichocarpa*)

The black cottonwood is distributed throughout the Sierra Nevada and coast range mountains from Canada to the Mexican border, reaching its best development in Washington and Oregon, where it attains a height of 100 to 200 feet and a diameter of 2 to 6 feet.

Form. The stem is straight, long, cylindrical, and clear of branches for one third to one half the total height; the crown is broadly oblong, open, and composed of coarse, upright branches. The root system is deep and spreading.

Occurrence. The black cottonwood thrives best in the deep, moist, open, fertile soils of river and cañon bottoms, where it is associated with the willows, alder, maple, and firs. It occasionally forms a pure stand, but usually occurs in mixture.

Distinctive characteristics. The black cottonwood may be distinguished by (1) the broadly oblong, pointed, firm, glossy, dark-green leaves, with slender, round stems; (2) the dense flowering catkins, from 1 to 3 inches long; (3) the large ($\frac{3}{4}$ inch long and $\frac{1}{4}$ inch in diameter), pointed, resinous, orange-brown buds; (4) the coarse, rather angled, orange-brown twigs; and (5) the thick, ashy-gray bark of old stems, broken into rounded ridges by deep fissures.

Wood. The wood is soft, light, moderately strong, of uniform texture, straight-grained, but is not durable; it seasons fairly well, works easily, and takes a fine finish.

The heartwood is a dull brown; the sapwood is thick and pale brown.

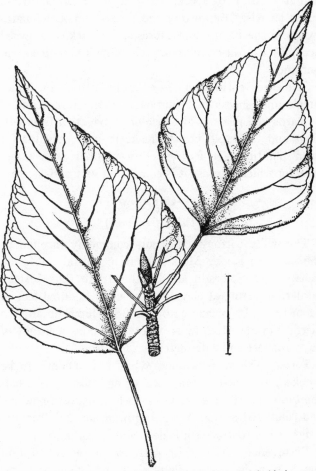

FIG. 84.   The arrowhead-shaped leaves and the pointed bud of the black cotton-wood.

Uses.   Black cottonwood is used for slack cooperage, woodenware, wagon stock, treatment posts, farm repairs, and fuel.   It is of special value in the manufacture of sugar barrels.   Because of the limited supply of hardwoods in the Pacific Coast forests, the black cottonwood occupies a position of relatively high commercial importance.

The black cottonwood is extensively used for windbreak and shelter-belt purposes in the protection of orchards and fields.   The ease of propagation from cuttings and the rapid growth make it of great value for farm planting.   It is frequently planted as a street tree, for which purpose it is considered very satisfactory.

WHITE COTTONWOOD

(*Populus fremontii*)

The white cottonwood occurs commonly throughout the southern Rocky Mountains from central California eastward to Colorado and southward to the Mexican border, occurring at elevations of a few hundred feet to 6000 feet.   It reaches its best development in the Sierra Nevada Mountains, where it attains a height of 80 to 100 feet and a diameter of 2 to 4 feet.

Form.   The stem is long, cylindrical, inclined to be crooked, and clear of branches for one third to one half the total height; the crown is open, broadly spreading, and composed of coarse, crooked branches and drooping twigs.   The root system is deep and spreading.

Occurrence.   The white cottonwood thrives best in the deep, moist, open soils of river and cañon bottoms, where it is associated with the willows, sycamore, birch, and alder. It occasionally occurs in small pure stands in cañon bottoms and about seeps.

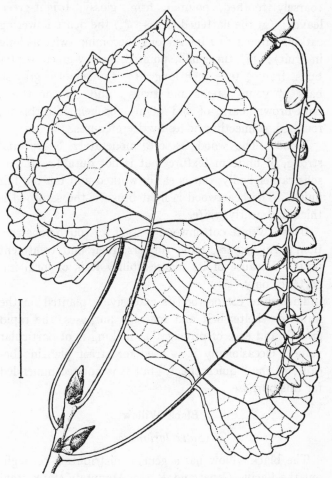

FIG. 85. The heart-shaped leaf and long cluster of seed pods of the white cottonwood.

Distinctive characteristics. The white cottonwood may be distinguished by (1) the broadly wedge-shaped, coarsely toothed, pointed, firm, glossy, bright-green leaves; (2) the flattened stems; (3) the dense flowering catkins, from 1 to 2 inches long (becoming twice as long in fruit); (4) the small, pointed, yellow-green winter buds, from $\frac{1}{4}$ to $\frac{1}{3}$ inch long; (5) the smooth, grayish bark of young stems and twigs; and (6) the thick, dark-brown bark of old stems, broken into broad, rounded, connecting ridges by deep fissures.

Wood. The wood is soft, moderately heavy and strong, of uniform texture, but is not durable; it seasons rather badly, but is easily worked and takes a fair finish. The heartwood is light brown; the sapwood is thick and nearly white.

Uses. White cottonwood is used for rough construction, farm repairs, mine timbers, fuel, and treatment posts. Because of its inaccessibility it is of local importance only.

The white cottonwood is extensively planted on the farm for shelter-belt and roadside purposes, the rapid growth and ease of propagation making it of particular value. Occasionally it is used for street planting because of the " quick effect," but it is not recommended for this purpose.

Black Willow

(*Salix lasiandra*)

The black willow has a general distribution throughout the Pacific Coast and Rocky Mountain states from Canada southward to the Mexican border, reaching its best development in Washington and Oregon, where it attains a height of 40 to 60 feet and a diameter of 20 to 30 inches.

Form. The stem is short, rather crooked, and clear of branches for one fourth to one third the total height; the crown is open, irregular, and composed of many small, upright branches. Over much of its range the growth is shrubby. The root system is shallow and spreading.

Occurrence. The black willow thrives best in the deep, moist, open, sandy or gravelly soils of stream bottoms and lake margins, where it is associated with cottonwood, sycamore, and alder.

Distinctive characteristics. The black willow may be distinguished by (1) the long, lance-pointed, finely toothed, yellow-green leaves, which are glossy on the upper sides and white on the lower sides; (2) the fine, reddish-brown twigs; (3) the thin ($\frac{1}{2}$ to $\frac{3}{4}$ inch), dark-brown or nearly black bark of old stems, broken into broad, rectangular, scaly plates by shallow longitudinal and cross fissures; and (4) the winter buds inclosed by a single scale.

Wood. The wood is light, soft, weak, brittle, dents without splitting, is moderately tough, but is not durable; it seasons well, works easily, and takes a fair finish. The heartwood is light brown; the sapwood is thick and nearly white.

Uses. Black willow is used for rough construction, farm repairs, treatment posts, fuel, and mine timbers. It is of considerable commercial value where it occurs in quantity.

The black willow is of great value in holding the

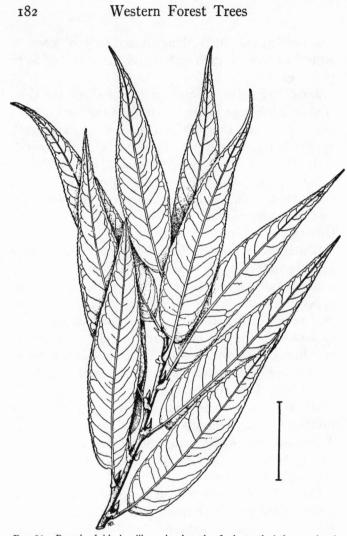

FIG. 86. Branch of black willow, showing the finely toothed, lance-pointed
leaves.

banks of streams in the prevention of erosion and is frequently planted along irrigation ditches and rivers for this purpose. It is sometimes used for windbreak purposes and for roadside planting, an occasional cutting back resulting in a dense growth of sprouts.

Palo Blanco or Hackberry[1]
(*Celtis reticulata*)

The palo blanco closely resembles the Mississippi hackberry or sugarberry of the Southern states. It is distributed throughout the southwestern United States from Texas to California, although it occurs nowhere in abundance. It occasionally attains a height of 40 to 50 feet and a diameter of 15 to 20 inches, but the average size is about 15 to 25 feet in height and 6 to 10 inches in diameter.

Form. The stem is short and often crooked; the crown is dense, bushy, and composed of short, stiff branches. Frequently it forms a dense shrubby growth without a distinct stem.

Occurrence. Palo blanco occurs most commonly as a cañon and arroyo tree of the desert ranges, occupying the dry, open, gravelly soils of stream bottoms and seeps. While it is usually found in mixture with aspen, birch, and some of the live oaks, it occasionally forms small pure stands in a park-like formation.

Distinctive characteristics. The palo blanco may be distinguished by (1) the dense, rounded crown; (2) the thick, leathery, wedge-shaped, lopsided, entire or indis-

---

[1] This species is considered by some to be a variety of *Celtis mississippiensis* and by others a variety of *Celtis occidentalis*. The U. S. Forest Service, however, lists it as a separate species.

tinctly toothed leaves, the upper sides of which are smooth and deep green and the lower sides roughened

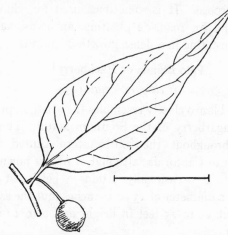

Fig. 87.　Leaf and fruit of the Palo blanco.　The leaf may be distinguished from that of the other hackberry by the absence of teeth, except near the tip.

by prominent veins and hairs and yellowish in color; (3) the orange-red, cherry-like fruit, occurring singly in the leaf axils in the autumn; and (4) the bluish-gray bark, broken into thin, short ridges.

Wood. The wood is rather soft and weak, light, close-grained, and not durable; it seasons well, is easily worked, and takes a fair polish. The heartwood is a pale greenish yellow; the sapwood is thick and white.

Uses. Because of its poor form the palo blanco is seldom used except for fuel purposes. When of sufficient size it is cut with associated species and manufactured for rough construction. It also possesses some value as a means of preventing wind and water erosion.

B. LEAVES WITH ENTIRE MARGIN

DESERT WILLOW   BEARBERRY
MOUNTAIN MAHOGANY   DOGWOOD
GUMS   CALIFORNIA LAUREL
                    MADROÑAS

Desert Willow or Flowering Willow

(*Chilopsis linearis*)

The desert willow has a general distribution throughout the southwestern United States from central California to Colorado and Texas, occurring at various elevations from sea level to 5000 feet. It reaches its best development in moist situations of the desert, where it attains a height of 20 to 40 feet and a diameter of 6 to 12 inches.

Form. The stem is more or less crooked, leaning, and clear of branches for one third to one half the total height; the crown is open, irregular, and more or less drooping. The root system is deep and spreading.

Occurrence. The desert willow thrives best in the deep, moist, well-drained, open soils of the desert and semi-desert regions of the Southwest, where it is associated with cottonwood, mesquite, and sagebrush. It frequently occurs in small, open, pure stands.

Distinctive characteristics. The desert willow may be distinguished by (1) the long, narrow, entire, pointed, willow-like leaves; (2) the terminal clusters of large, showy, catalpa-like flowers; (3) the long, round, catalpa-like pod, containing the winged seeds; and (4) the thick, dark-brown bark of old stems, broken into broad connected ridges by narrow fissures.

FIG. 88.   Desert willow.   Spike of showy flowers, a seed pod (behind the flower spike), and seeds (lower right-hand corner).

Wood. The wood is soft, light, weak, brittle, but durable; it seasons well, works easily, and takes a fair finish. The heartwood is a yellow-brown; the sapwood is thick and pale yellow.

Uses. Desert willow is of considerable local importance for fencing purposes. It is also used for general farm repairs and for fuel.

The desert willow is an attractive ornamental shrub or small tree and is commonly used throughout the southern United States in park and yard group plantings. It thrives under a wide range of soil and moisture conditions. The combination of catalpa-like blossoms and willow-like leaves is quite a novelty to one not familiar with the tree.

Mountain Mahogany

(Cercocarpus ledifolius)

The mountain mahogany occurs commonly throughout the Rocky Mountain system from Canada to the Mexican border at elevations of 5000 to 10,000 feet. It reaches its best development in the semi-desert mountain ranges of the Great Basin, where it attains a height of 20 to 30 feet and a diameter (at the ground) of 1 to 2 feet.

Form. The stem is short, crooked, tapering, and clear of branches for 2 to 6 feet; the crown is open, flat, and spreading, the stiff, contorted branches meeting the stem at right angles. The taproot penetrates deeply into the earth.

Occurrence. The mountain mahogany occupies the deep, open, gravelly or stony soils of the high foothills, where it occurs in extensive, open, pure stands or in mixture with the desert junipers and piñon pines. Occasionally it is found in the cañon bottoms, but the growth there is no better than on the ridge tops.

Distinctive characteristics. The mountain mahog-

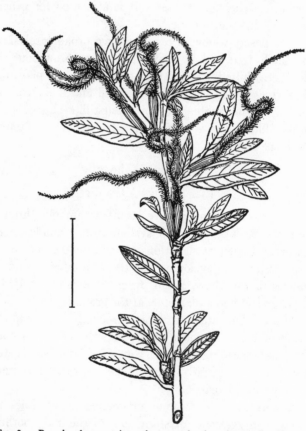

FIG. 89. Branch of mountain mahogany, showing the small, oblong, pointed leaves and the peculiar tailed fruit.

any may be distinguished by (1) the small, oblong, pointed, persistent, entire (or indistinctly and irregularly toothed), dull grayish-green leaves, the edges of which are more or less incurving; (2) the peculiar fruit, composed of a single seed, about the size of an oat grain, to which is attached a long, hairy, corkscrew-like tail; (3) the thin, tight, smooth, grayish bark of young stems and branches; (4) the moderately thick, grayish red-brown bark of old stems, broken into broad, plate-like ridges by shallow fissures; and (5) the open, squat form and drab appearance.

Wood. The wood is heavy, hard, dense, strong, brittle, and durable; it seasons poorly, checks badly, is difficult to work, but takes a fine finish. The heartwood is a bright mahogany-red; the sapwood is thin and pale yellow.

Uses. Mountain mahogany is very valuable for fuel purposes. Occasionally it is used for cabinetwork and farm repairs, and in the manufacture of novelties and roller-skate wheels. Its use is limited by its poor form and inaccessibility.

Mountain mahogany is of great value in the protection of watersheds from wind and water erosion.

The Gums (*Eucalyptus*)

The gums, of which there are a large number, occur naturally in Australia only. About forty kinds are being used in experimental plantings in California to determine their suitability to conditions of the arid Southwest. The blue gum was introduced about 1860 and its range is quite generally determined by artificial and natural plantings. Some of the newer introductions are more frost-hardy than the blue gum and many are more drought-resistant.

The gums are characterized by persistent, smooth-margined leaves, which vary from nearly round to lance-shaped and sickle-shaped forms. The fruit consists of a valved, woody cup, which may be deep or shallow. The bark of twigs and small stems is thin, smooth, and greenish to reddish or brownish in color. The growth is exceedingly rapid, especially when one considers the high technical value of the wood, trees in plantations attaining fence-post size in three years and crosstie size in seven years.

The wood of the different gums varies from hard to soft and from dark, mahogany tints to nearly white. Some of the woods are of as high commercial value as hickory, ash, and oak, while others are quite inferior. In general, the wood is cross-grained and very difficult to work except when green.

KEY TO THE GUMS

A. **Bark of branches and young stems blue-green, smooth** . . . BLUE GUM (*E. globulus*)
B. **Bark of branches and young stems reddish** . . . . RED GUM (*E. rostrata*)
C. **Bark of branches and young stems greenish or grayish** . . SUGAR GUM (*E. corynocalyx*)

BLUE GUM

(*Eucalyptus globulus*)

The blue gum has been planted extensively through-out the southwestern United States where the minimum temperature does not fall below 20° F., and occurs naturally at various elevations from sea level to 6000 feet. It is a common tree of the irrigated sections of central and southern California, southern Arizona, and portions of New Mexico and Texas. Under favorable conditions it attains a height of 125 to 150 feet and a diameter of 3 to 4 feet in thirty years.

Form. The stem of the plantation-grown tree is long, straight, cylindrical, and clear of branches for one half to two thirds the total height; the crown is spreading and rounded. In the open the branches are retained to a point near the ground and the crown is broadly rounded. (See Frontispiece, also Figure 2.) The drooping twigs give the tree a "weeping" form. The root system is deep and spreading.

Occurrence. The blue gum thrives best in the deep, moist, well-drained, loamy soils of the coast region where the minimum annual precipitation is about 15 inches. It thrives under irrigation in the interior valleys where the temperature is mildly subtropical, but does poorly under arid tropical conditions.

Distinctive characteristics. The blue gum may be distinguished by (1) the glossy, dark-green, sickle-shaped leaves; (2) the angular twigs; (3) the thin, smooth, bluish-green bark of young stems and branches; (4) the thin, ragged, grayish-brown bark of old stems, the bark flaking away in long strips (see Figure 10); (5) the white flowers borne in the axils of the leaves; and (6) the four-valved (sometimes three- or five-valved), woody, cup-shaped fruit.

Wood. The wood is heavy, hard, strong, dense, **very**

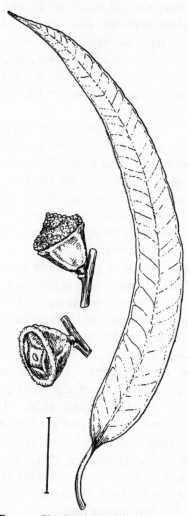

FIG. 90. The long, sickle-shaped leaf and
the fruiting pods of the blue gum.

tough, of uniform texture, has an uneven wavy grain, and is moderately durable; it seasons poorly, is difficult to work, but takes a high finish. The heartwood is yellowish to pale brown; the sapwood is thick and white.

Uses. Blue gum has displaced oak for many purposes. It is used for wagon stock, agricultural implements, insulator pins, marine piling, flooring, treatment posts, crossties, general construction, and fuel.

The leaves are distilled in the production of oil of eucalyptus, a valuable medicinal material.

The blue gum is. extensively planted for windbreak purposes in the citrus regions of California, the evergreen character of the tree giving year-round protection. The tree is also used generally for ornamental purposes, the open, spreading crown and the ragged bark proving most attractive. Under irrigation conditions the growth is very rapid; seedlings sometimes attain a height of 15 to 20 feet in one year.

RED GUM

(*Eucalyptus rostrata*)

The red gum has been planted quite generally throughout the more tropical sections of the southwestern United States and has made a good growth under the hot, droughty conditions of the Imperial Valley. Experimental plantings indicate that it is more frost-resistant than blue gum and that it will also withstand alkali conditions.

Forms. In plantation-grown trees the stem is long, more or less crooked, and clear of branches for one half to two thirds the total height; the crown is open, spread-

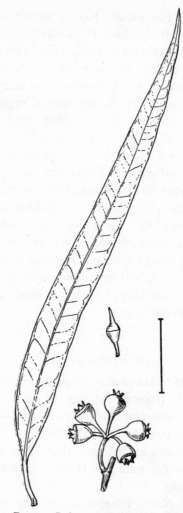

FIG. 91. Red gum. Compare the leaf
and fruit with those of the blue gum (Fig.
90) and the sugar gum (Fig. 92).

ing, and rather irregular. In the open the branches persist to a point near the ground. The root system is deep and spreading.

Occurrence. The red gum thrives best in the deep, open, irrigated soils of the interior valleys, but will maintain itself in comparatively dry situations when once established. It is better adapted to semi-arid conditions than any other member of the group.

Distinctive characteristics. The red gum may be distinguished by (1) the long, narrow, lance-pointed, more or less sickle-shaped, glossy, green leaves; (2) the smooth, reddish twigs; (3) the thick, dark-gray bark of old stems, broken into ragged ridges by deep fissures or sloughing away in long strips; (4) the large clusters of white blossoms; and (5) the clusters of four-valved fruits, which have protruding valve tips.

Wood. The wood is heavy, hard, strong, tough, dense, even-textured, cross-grained, and durable; it seasons badly, is difficult to work, but takes a fine finish. The heartwood is reddish to dark red; the sapwood is thick and pale red.

Uses. The wood is considered to be somewhat inferior to that of the blue gum, but it is used for much the same purposes. Because of the color the wood is more often used for interior finishing, flooring, furniture, and cabinetwork. It is also used for fencing, crossties, marine piling, and fuel.

The red gum is attractive as an ornamental tree and is extensively used in windbreak plantings throughout its range.

Sugar Gum

(Eucalyptus corynocalyx)

The sugar gum will withstand a somewhat lower temperature than the blue gum and should have a more extended distribution. At present it is planted throughout the semi-arid regions of the southwestern United States. Under irrigation the growth is as rapid as that of the blue gum.

Form. In the plantation-grown tree the stem is long, straight, and clear of branches for one half to two thirds the total height; the crown is very open, spreading, and rather irregular. In the open the branches are retained to a point near the ground. The root system is deep and spreading.

Occurrence. The sugar gum thrives best under conditions which are most favorable to the blue gum but is somewhat more drought-resistant. Once established by irrigation, it will make a fair growth even in relatively dry situations.

Distinctive characteristics. The sugar gum may be distinguished by (1) the long, narrow, more or less curved, lance-shaped leaves, which are dark green on the upper surface and pale green on the lower surface; (2) the clusters of white blossoms; (3) the clusters of egg-shaped, three-valved (occasionally four-valved) fruit; (4) the smooth, greenish or reddish twigs; and (5) the scaly, deciduous, creamy or grayish bark of old stems.

Wood. The wood is heavy, hard, strong, tough, dense, of even texture, irregular grain, and durable; it seasons poorly, is difficult to work, but takes a fine

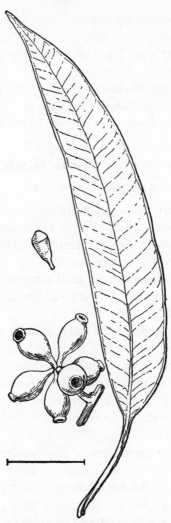

FIG. 92. Sugar gum. Compare leaf,
fruit cluster, and seed with those of the
other gums.

finish. The heartwood is pale yellow; the sapwood is thick and white.

Uses. Sugar gum has the same uses as blue gum (see page 193).

The sugar gum is extensively planted for windbreak and ornamental purposes. Because of the more open character of the crown it is frequently preferred to blue gum.

Bearberry or Cascara Sagrada

(*Rhamnus purshiana*)

The bearberry has a general distribution throughout the Pacific Coast and the Rocky Mountain states from Canada southward to the Mexican border, occurring at various elevations from sea level to 8000 feet. It reaches its best development in Washington and Idaho, where it attains a height of 30 to 40 feet and a diameter of 15 to 20 inches.

Form. In the forest the stem is long, straight, and clear of branches for one half the total height; the crown is open, rounded, and composed of numerous horizontal branches. In the open the stem is short and thick and the crown is full and rounded. At high elevations the growth is shrubby. The root system is spreading.

Distinctive characteristics. The bearberry may be distinguished by (1) the oblong, rather rectangular, fine-toothed, parallel lateral-veined, hairy, grayish- or bluish-green leaves; (2) the cherry-like, purple, juicy fruits, borne in clusters of two or three in the axils of the leaves, containing two or three hard, smooth, green,

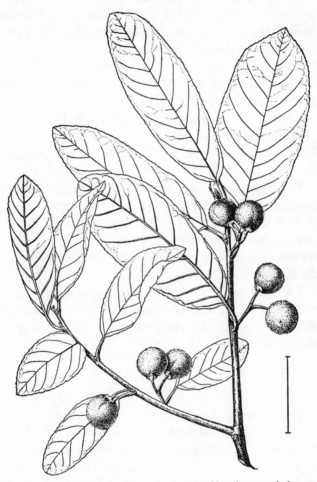

FIG. 93. Branch of the bearberry, showing the oblong leaves and clusters
of smooth, round fruits.

coffee-like seeds; (3) the slender, hairy, yellow-green to reddish-brown twigs; (4) the thin, grayish-brown bark of old stems, broken into loose scales; and (5) the bitter taste of the twigs and inner bark.

Wood. The wood is moderately heavy, firm, brittle, coarse-grained, but not durable; it seasons well, works easily, and takes a fair finish. The heartwood is a pale yellow-brown; the sapwood is thick and white.

Uses. Because of the poor form the bearberry is of little value from the standpoint of the lumber producer. It is used locally for fuel.

The bitter inner bark is collected in the commercial production of cascara, which is used medicinally. The trees that are destroyed for the bark are replaced by a heavy growth of stump sprouts. The new growth should be managed conservatively for continued production.

The bearberry is of attractive appearance and is used in both the United States and Europe for ornamental purposes. Its chief value for this use is as a high-growing shrub.

Dogwood

(*Cornus nuttallii*)

The dogwood has a general distribution throughout the Pacific Coast region from Canada to the Mexican border, occurring at various elevations from sea level to about 6000 feet. It reaches its best development in western Washington and Oregon, where it attains a height of 50 to 100 feet and a diameter of 1 to 2 feet.

Form. The stem of the forest-grown tree is long, straight, cylindrical, and clear of branches for one half to two thirds the total height; the crown is narrow, oblong, and composed of short, ascending branches. In the open the stem is short and the crown full and rounded. The root system is deep and spreading.

Occurrence. The dogwood thrives best in the deep, moist, fresh, well-drained, fertile soils of stream bottoms, coves, cañons, and mountain slopes, where it is associated with the redwood, Douglas fir, hemlock, maple, alder, and sugar pine. It never occurs in a pure stand.

Distinctive characteristics. The dogwood may be distinguished by (1) the large, oval, pointed, hairy, thin, bright-green leaves, the lower sides of which are silvery and hairy; (2) the lateral veins, running more or less parallel with the margin; (3) the heads of small flowers, surrounded by the large, white, petal-like involucre; (4) the clusters of orange-red, fleshy, bitter fruits, which persist all winter; (5) the thin, smooth, ashy-brown or reddish bark of young stems and branches; and (6) the dark-brown bark of old stems, broken into small square plates by deep fissures.

Wood. The wood is heavy, hard, strong, very dense, tough, of uniform texture, but not durable; it is difficult to season, difficult to work, but takes a fine finish. The heartwood is a light reddish brown; the sapwood is thick and pale brown.

Uses. Dogwood is used for farm repairs, tool handles, wood turning, cabinetwork, rough construction, and fuel. Its use is limited by the small supply.

The dogwood is a beautiful ornamental tree and is much used in plantings of all kinds. The pink-flowering varieties are most attractive. Its ability to thrive in dense shade makes it of value for use about the house or in the shade of other trees.

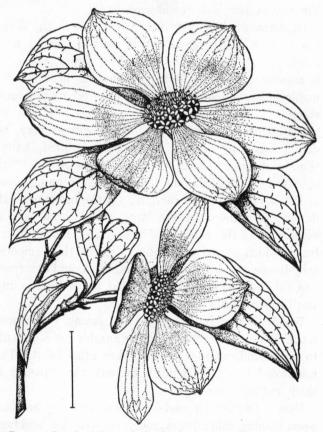

FIG. 94 Branch of dogwood, showing heads of true flowers surrounded by the large, white, petal-like involucre.

California Laurel, Bay Tree, or Myrtle

(*Umbellularia californica*)

The California laurel has a general distribution throughout the Pacific Slope from Oregon southward to the Mexican border, occurring at various elevations from sea level to 4000 feet. It reaches its maximum development in southwestern Oregon, where it attains a height of 50 to 100 feet and a diameter of 2 to 5 feet.

Form. The stem of the forest-grown tree is long, straight, and clear of branches for one third to one half the total height; the crown is dense, narrow, and composed of numerous ascending branches. In the open the stem is short and thick and the crown is spreading and rounded. The root system is spreading.

Occurrence. The California laurel thrives best in the deep, moist, open soils of stream bottoms and sheltered mountain slopes, where it is associated with maple, alder, yew, sycamore, madroña, and the oaks. In dry situations and at high elevations it forms a shrubby growth.

Distinctive characteristics. The California laurel may be distinguished by (1) the oblong, pointed, persistent, thick, glossy, deep yellow-green leaves, the undersides of which are a paler green; (2) the aromatic, camphorlike odor of the crushed leaves; (3) the olive-like, yellow-green, single-seeded fruit, with its thin, leathery skin; (4) the moderately thick, scaly, dark-brown bark; and (5) the dense, broadly rounded crown.

Wood. The wood is heavy, hard, moderately strong, dense, fine-grained, of uniform texture, but not durable;

it seasons poorly, is difficult to work, but takes a fine finish. The heartwood is a rich yellow-brown; the sapwood is thick and pale brown. Beautifully mottled effects in the wood are not uncommon.

FIG. 95.   Leaves and olive-like fruit of the California laurel.

Uses. California laurel is used for interior finishing, furniture, flooring, cabinetwork, parquetry, wood turning, novelties, and farm repairs. The demand is limited by the small supply.

The leaves are used in cookery and in the distillation of a medicinal oil. Occasionally the fruit is distilled in the production of umbellic acid.

The California laurel is a most attractive ornamental tree and is extensively planted throughout its native region. It is easily grown from seed and stands transplanting well.

The Madroñas (*Arbutus*)

KEY TO THE MADROÑAS

A. **Leaves oblong, entire or toothed**
    (both kinds on same tree) . . . MADROÑA (*A. menziesii*)
B. **Leaves lance-pointed, entire** . . MANZANITA (*A. xalapensis*)

MADROÑA OR LAUREL

(*Arbutus menziesii*)

The madroña is distributed quite generally over the Pacific Slope from Canada southward to the Mexican border, occurring at various elevations from sea level to 5000 feet. It reaches its best development in the redwood region of northern California, where it attains a height of 80 to 100 feet and a diameter of 2 to 5 feet.

Form. Under the most favorable conditions the stem is long, straight, and clear of branches for one half to two thirds the total height; the crown is broad, rounded, and flattened. In the open the stem is short and the crown is full and rounded. At high elevations

and in the southern part of its range the growth is
shrubby.

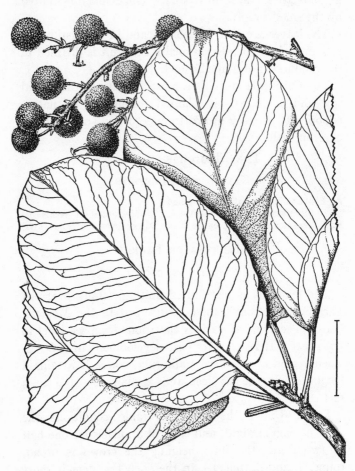

FIG. 96. Madrona. Below, leaf branch, showing the large, oblong leaves;
above, cluster of berry-like fruits.

Occurrence. The madroña thrives best in the deep, moist, open, well-drained, fertile soils of river bottoms, mountain valleys, cañons, and protected slopes, where it is associated with the redwood, tanbark oak, laurel, chinquapin, Douglas fir, maple, and yellow pine. Occasionally it forms small, pure stands.

Distinctive characteristics. The madroña may be distinguished by (1) the thin, papery, chestnut-brown bark of old trees, breaking and curling away from the tree; (2) the thin, tight, smooth, red bark of young stems and branches; (3) the large, thick, entire, oblong, leathery, smooth, dark-green leaves, which are hairy and whitish on the undersides; (4) the terminal spikes of white, fragrant flowers, resembling lilies of the valley; and (5) the clusters of orange-red, cherry-like fruits, half an inch in diameter.

Wood. The wood is heavy, hard, strong, rather brittle, fine-grained, of uniform texture, but not durable; it seasons well, is moderately easy to work, and takes a fine finish. The heartwood is a light reddish brown; the sapwood is thick and white.

Uses. Madroña is used for interior finishing, furniture, flooring, cabinetwork, wagon stock, and fuel. It is frequently substituted for mahogany.

The bark is rich in tannic acid and is occasionally peeled for this purpose. As an ornamental tree the madroña stands in the first rank; the dark-green, shiny foliage, the striking flowers and fruit, and the contrasting red bark furnish a picture which the observer long remembers with pleasure.

Manzanita or Madroña

(*Arbutus xalapensis*)

The manzanita is found, at elevations of 6000 to 8000 feet, throughout the southern portions of Texas and Arizona, extending southward into Mexico. It reaches its best development in the protected mountain cañons, where it attains a height of 20 to 30 feet and a diameter of 6 to 12 inches. It is closely related to the madroña (*Arbutus menziesii*).

Form. The stem is usually short, crooked, and clear of branches for but a few feet above ground; the crown is dense, spreading, rounded, and consists of several large, contorted branches. Frequently it takes the form of a large, irregular shrub. The root system is deep and spreading.

Occurrence. The manzanita thrives best in a deep, moist, well-drained, open soil, but is crowded out of the better situations by more tolerant trees. Usually it occupies the dry limestone ridges and gravelly benches at high elevations, where it is associated with the piñon pines and desert junipers. Frequently it occurs in extensive pure stands.

Distinctive characteristics. The manzanita may be distinguished by (1) the thick, glossy, persistent, oval, entire (or coarsely and irregularly toothed), dark-green leaves; (2) the clusters of white blossoms (resembling those of the lily of the valley), on reddish stems; (3) the thin, smooth, red bark of young stems and branches; (4) the thin ($\frac{1}{2}$ inch), dark reddish-brown bark of old stems, broken into thick, plate-like scales by shallow fissures; and (5) the clusters of dark orange-red fruits, with sweetish flesh.

Wood. The wood is heavy, hard, moderately strong, rather brittle, close-grained, but not durable; it seasons poorly, but works easily and takes a fine finish. The heartwood is a light brown, tinged with red; the sapwood is thin and pale brown.

Uses. Manzanita is used for farm repairs, fuel, mine timbers, handle stock, and rough construction. The bark is sometimes used for tanning leather.

References

Silvical Leaflets, Forest Service, U. S. D. A. (See Price List issued by Superintendent of Documents.)

Bulletin, Forest Service, U. S. D. A., " The Junipers of the Rocky Mountain Region."

Bulletin, Forest Service, U. S. D. A., " The Cypresses of the Rocky Mountain Region."

Circular 59, Forest Service, U. S. D. A., " Eucalyptus."

Circular 72, Forest Service, U. S. D. A., " Western Yellow Pine."

Special Publication, Forest Service, U. S. D. A., " Trees of the Pacific Slope."

Bulletin, New Mexico Agricultural Experiment Station, " Trees and Shrubs of New Mexico."

Bulletin 22, University of Texas, " The Trees of Texas."

Bulletin, State Forester, California, " Third Biennial Report, 1910 " (description of chaparral and native trees of California).

Bulletin, University of California Experiment Station, " Eucalyptus in California."

Bulletin, California State Board of Forestry, " Handbook for Eucalyptus Planters."

" Important Timber Trees of the United States," Elliott, S. B. (Houghton Mifflin Company, Boston; 1912.)

" American Forest Trees," Gibson, H. H. (Hardwood Record, Ellsworth Building, Chicago; 1913.)

" Manual of Trees of North America," Sargent, C. S. (Houghton Mifflin Company, Boston; 1905.)

APPENDIX (1966)

Comments and Suggestions. In the following paragraphs, modern names, both common and scientific, will be used with page reference to the tree in question, and some additional information will be added where it may be helpful in identification.

Page 28-29. In this key, and later in the text, it should be noted that Big Tree or Sierra Redwood has short, sharp and awl-like needles in spiral arrangement and not scale-like as indicated in the heading; also, California Nutmeg and Western Yew have long, slender, needle-like leaves and so should not be classified under the scale-like heading.

Page 31. In the key to the Pines, the following additions may be helpful:
Needles in bundles of 5.
1. Needles short, upturned and crowded. High mountain trees.
    Limber Pine, *P. flexilis*, Rockies, Cascades and Sierra. (p. 31)
    Bristlecone Pine, *P. aristata*, S. Rockies and White Mts.
    Whitebark Pine, *P. albicaulis*, Wyo. and Mont. to Cent. Calif.
    Foxtail Pine, *P. balfouriana*, Mts. of N. and Cent. Calif.
2. Needles longer and more slender. Timber trees of middle elev.
    Western White Pine, *P. monticola*, Idaho, W. Mont. to Cent. Calif.; lower elev. in Wash. and Oreg. (p. 34)
    Sugar Pine, *P. lambertiana*. Cent. Oreg. in mts. to S. Calif.; not in Wash. Largest of all pine trees.
3. Needles stout and very long. Coastal in San Diego Co., Calif.
    Torrey Pine, *P. torreyana*.
4. Introduced species as ornamentals:
    Eastern White Pine, *P. strobus* from N.E. North America.
    Himalayan or Bhotan Pine, *P. excelsa* (wallichinana) from India.
    Montezuma Pine, *P. montezumae*, Mexico.
Needles in bundles of 4.
    Parry Pinyon, *P. quadrifolia*, A rare and local pinyon pine of Calif. and adjacent Mexico.

Needles in bundles of 3. Calif. species.

1. Needles very long, heavy cones open when mature.

   Coulter or Big-cone Pine, *P. coulteri*, cones with stout, hooked spurs, yellow-brown, seeds with long wings. S. Calif. (p. 41)

   Digger Pine, *P. sabiniana*, cones 10 in. or less, chocolate-brown with shorter spurs, seeds with short wings. Foothills. (p. 45)

2. Needles short and slender, cones smaller, curved and persist in whorls on stem and branches unopened.

   Knobcone Pine, *P. attenuata*. Tree of poor form on shallow soils in scattered areas; one of the fire-type pines.

3. Introduced species.

   Canary Island Pine. *P. canariensis*, a beautiful tree with long, yellow-green needles and tall, conical form which grows well in mild areas along the Calif. coast. Not frost hardy.

Needles in bundles of 3 and 2, usually 3.

1. Needles long, cones symmetrical with spiny tips on cone-scales. Important and large timber trees of mountain areas.

   Ponderosa Pine, *P. ponderosa*, needles yellow-green, cones to 5 in. Most widely distributed and important timber pine of western America. Middle elev. in B.C., S. Dakota, S. to W. Texas through Cascades and Sierra to Mexico. (p. 40)

   Jeffrey Pine, *P. jeffreyi*, needles blue-green but very similar, cones larger and bark with vanilla-like fragrance. Usually at higher elev. from S.W. Oreg. to S. Calif.

2. Needles short and slender, dark blue-green; cones unsymmetrical, borne in whorls and some remaining closed for years. Coastal Calif.

   Monterey Pine, *P. radiata*, the world's fastest growing pine, extensively planted in Australia, New Zealand, South America and Africa. Native only S. of San Francisco Bay, but grows well along the coast to Cent. Oreg. and is being tried even farther for pulp and timber. Also grown for a Christmas tree in plantations along the coast.

Needles in bundles of 2.

Digger Pine, *P. sabiniana* should not be included here (see above).

1a. Needles short, cones small and unsymmetrical with small seeds and spiny prickles on scales.

   Lodgepole Pine, *P. contorta var. murrayana* of some authors. Widespread distribution at higher elev. from S. Alaska and Alberta to Wyo., N. Utah and Colo. Merges in Wash. and B.C into a smaller coastal tree called Beach Pine found near the coast from N. Calif. to Alaska. (p. 48)

1b. Needles short, cones small and symmetrical, seeds large, edible. Distribution S. Rockies and in S.W. Ariz., New Mex. and W. Texas.

Pinyon Pine, *P. edulis* is the 2-needle nut pine; one of the four pinyons which yield delicious edible seeds. (p. 51)

2. Needles longer, more slender and bluish green; cones larger, with stout mitre-like cone-scales, some remaining closed for years.

Bishop Pine, *P. muricata*, a coastal species native from Santa Barbara Co. to Humboldt Co., Calif., reaching its largest size at the north. Resembles Monterey Pine; grown in limited amounts as a Christmas tree.

3. Introduced species, planted as ornamentals and for Christmas trees.

Scot's Pine, *P. sylvestris*, from Europe, important as a Christmas tree.

Austrian Pine, *P. nigra*, occasional in Christmas tree plantings.

Italian Stone Pine, *P. pinea*, from the Mediterranean, a spreading tree with a broad umbrella-shaped crown; ornamental.

Aleppo Pine, *P. halepensis*, from eastern Mediterranean with gray bark, slender light-green needles and stalked persistent cones.

Japanese Black Pine, *P. thunbergii*, a favorite ornamental.

Japanese Red Pine, *P. densiflora*, much branched ornamental with slender needles and small, persistent cones.

Cluster or Maritime Pine, *P. pinaster* from the Mediterranean; stiff, dark-green needles. Occasional as an ornamental.

Swiss Mountain Pine, *P. mugo* and vars. from Europe. Short, dark needles and tiny cones. A favorite dwarf ornamental.

Needles borne singly, but having basal sheath of scales.

Single-leaf Pinyon Pine, *Pinus monophylla*, an important nut pine of the Great Basin area from S. Idaho to N.W. Ariz. and S. Calif. A chief food source of Indian tribes. (p 52)

Page 54. Western Larch, *Larix occidentalis*, now rarely referred to as Red Fir.

Subalpine Larch, *Larix lyallii*, a very similar deciduous larch from high mountain areas of Wash., N. Idaho and W. Mont. and in adjacent Canada. Not a commercial species.

Page 57. Western Hemlock, *Tsuga heterophylla*, a valuable and very beautiful timber tree of the Pacific Northwest to N.W. coastal Calif. Very difficult to grow in cultivation outside its natural range.

Mountain Hemlock, *Tsuga mertensiana*, also known as Black Hemlock; a mountain tree of high elev. from Cent. Calif. through Oreg., Wash. and B.C. to S. Alaska. Now being cut to some extent in the Pacific Northwest for lumber and for shipment of logs to Japan.

Page 59. Coast Redwood, *Sequoia sempervirens*, the large and very important timber species of the Calif. coastal area from Cent. Monterey Co. to a small area in S. W. Oreg. Originally covered an area of about 1½ million acres; the world's tallest tree (365 ft.) ; some specimens have reached an age of 2200 yrs. Produces fine-grained and very durable lumber. Some 60,000 acres have been set aside for this species in the Calif. State Park System. Notable also for rapidity of growth as a young tree. Fully stocked stands on good soil have grown at the rate of 2,000 board ft. per acre per year for 60 to 80 yrs.

INTRODUCED: Dawn Redwood, *Metasequoia glyptostroboides*, a deciduous member of the redwood family from China which has been grown in recent years as an interesting ornamental. Has smaller cones than coast redwood and light green foliage with opposite branching. Can be easily propagated from cuttings.

Sugi or Japanese Cryptomeria, *Cryptomeria japonica*, a tree from Japan which quite closely resembles coast redwood in bark, foliage and wood characteristics. Grows well under similar climatic conditions and is in occasional use as a garden ornamental in Calif. There are several named varieties.

Note: for Sierra Redwood, *Sequoia gigantea*, see p. 97.

Page 61. Douglas Fir, *Pseudotsuga menziesii* (taxifolia) with its great size, excellent quality lumber and wide geographic distribution is now the most important timber tree in both the U.S. and Canada. Has become most important wood in the manufacture of high quality plywood. Reproduces well as a young tree and thousands of acres are managed as permanently productive forest lands under the Tree Farm System. Also the most widely used Christmas tree throughout western America. These are produced from "farmed" natural stands of second growth, and also from intensively managed plantations.

Big-cone Douglas Fir, *Pseudotsuga macrocarpa*, a tree of very similar characteristics, foliage and bark, but with much larger cones. Not a commercial species; confined to a few mountain canyon areas of S. Calif.

Page 64. The key to the Firs should be considered with the following modifications under each species:

California Red Fir, *Abies magnifica*, a mountain tree of large size and excellent quality lumber usually found at elev. above 5,000 ft. from Cent. Oreg. S. to the Cent. Sierras and at upper elev. in the coast ranges in N. Calif. Its bark when cut shows blood red color. Its four-angled needles are usually sharply upturned and usually have a bright blue-green color. This with the smooth, silvery-gray upper bark and the fine, conical symmetry of young trees has given it great popularity and value as the "Silver-tip" Christmas tree. Its large, erect and barrel-shaped cones have bracts which are shorter than the cone-scales, but in the following, they are longer and "feathered," similar to those of Noble Fir.

Shasta Red Fir, *Abies magnifica var. shastensis*, has the same range, similar in all characteristics to the above, except for the long, decurved cone-scale bracts which make this variety virtually indistinguishable from Noble Fir which has a more northerly range in mts. of Oreg., Wash. and B.C.

Page 66. Noble Fir, *Abies procera*, a very similar and valuable fir of upper elev. in coast ranges of the Pacific Northwest to S.W. Oreg., but it is not known to occur in Calif. Its dark furrowed trunk bark is flinty and shows blood-red color when cut, as in the above species. Its young bark is smooth and marked by balsam blisters, as are all the other firs, and the conical symmetry of the young tree makes it one of the preferred Christmas trees.

Pacific Silver Fir, *Abies amabilis*, a large and handsome fir of the coast range mountain country at upper elev. from S. Alaska through B.C., Wash. and Oreg. to about the Calif. state line. Deep green needles with silvery lower sides, smooth gray bark on the upper stem and large, barrel-shaped, upright cones. Foliage with notched tips more closely resembles that of eastern Balsam Fir than that of other western firs. Now being cut for lumber and for foreign shipment of logs. Young trees in demand as Christmas trees.

Page 69. Subalpine or Alpine Fir, *Abies lasiocarpa*, a timber-line tree with wide distribution in higher mountain areas from Alaska S. to Oreg. and E. to Idaho, W. Wyo. and W. Mont. and the Rockies to Colo., W. New Mex. and W. Ariz. Tall and slender in form but of moderate size and not often cut for lumber. In the S. Rockies it has a distinctive variety:

Corkbark Fir, *Abies lasiocarpa var. arizonica*, distinguished by very handsome, soft blue-green foliage and thin corky bark on the main trunk. Occurs in Ariz. with associated large trees of Aspen, which constitutes one of the most beautiful forests in the west.

Page 71. White Fir, *Abies concolor*, a large tree with a very extensive range at middle elev. from Idaho and W. Wyo. through E. Oreg. and down the Sierra to northern Mexico. Now an important timber species with good capacity for reproduction and a good rate of growth after a slow start for about 15 years. Young trees find a good market as Christmas trees and are being grown in plantations for this purpose. Now being extensively used for

216 **Western Forest Trees**

pulp and paper as well as for lumber.

Page 74. Grand Fir or Lowland Fir, *Abies grandis*, a tree of lowland and lower elev. areas from Sonoma Co., Calif. N. in coastal mts. to S. British Columbia and E. to N.E. Oreg., E. Wash., Idaho and W. Mont. Becomes a large tree with fine dark green crown and in many areas is now utilized for lumber, pulp and paper and other forest products. Not found in the Calif. Sierra.

ADDED: Bristlecone Fir, *Abies bracteata* (venusta), has the most restricted range of any American fir, being found only at high elev. in the Santa Lucia mts. of Monterey Co., Calif. Long, quite broad and sharp-pointed buds and egg-shaped cones which resemble Medusa heads because of the long, slender bracts protruding from the cone-scales. Occasionally cultivated as an ornamental.

INTRODUCED: Nordmann Fir, *Abies nordmanniana* from Asia Minor.

Spanish Fir, *Abies pinsapo* from Spain; sharp, spruce-like needles.

Momi Fir, *Abies firma* from Japan; broad needles, notched tips.

Greek Fir, *Abies cephalonica*, from Greece; long, sharp needles, 7 in. cones.

Page 79. Engelmann Spruce, *Picea engelmannii* is not known as White Spruce. An important timber species of interior mts. from Canada to Mexico. Slender and less sharp needles than the following.

Page 81. Blue or Colorado Blue Spruce, *Picea pungens* (parryana), a hardy and beautiful spruce from the S. Rockies with striking blue-gray sharp needles: slow growing in youth, but widely used as an attractive ornamental throughout the west.

INTRODUCED: Norway Spruce, *Picea abies* (excelsa) from Europe, with dark green conical crown of short, soft needles and large pendant cones. Many ornamental varieties quite commonly planted.

INTRODUCED: White Spruce, *Picea glauca* from N.E. North America with gray-green foliage and small tan cones; grown as a Christmas tree.

Himalayan Spruce, *Picea smithiana* from India; has a thin crown of long, slender needles on pendant twigs. Occasional.

Oriental Spruce, *Picea orientalis*, from Asia Minor; has very short, soft and very dark green needles and small cones.

Page 84. "Trees with Scale-like Leaves." Eliminate from this classification Sierra Redwood, California Nutmeg and Western Yew as indicated above.

The False Cypresses—genus Chamaecyparis.

Alaska or Nootka Cedar, *Chamaecyparis nootkatensis* found from Alaska at gradually increasing elev. in coastal mountain country to about the Oreg.-Calif. line. Several horticultural varieties.

Appendix

Port Orford Cedar or Lawson Cypress, *Chamaecyparis lawsoniana* has been a very important timber tree in a restricted coastal area from Coos Co., Oreg. S. to the Klamath and Trinity rivers in N. Calif. In the Coos Co. area it has now been attacked by a fungus disease which makes its future uncertain in this moist area of its former maximum development. In wide use as an attractive ornamental. Several horticultural varieties.

Page 89. Western Red Cedar or Giant Arborvitae, *Thuja plicata*, the large timber tree of the Pacific Northwest. Several landscape forms used in ornamental planting.

INTRODUCED: Northern White Cedar, *Thuja occidentalis* of N.E. North America, present in most areas as a decorative ornamental with many landscape forms (slender erect, globe, golden, dwarf, etc.). Oriental or Chinese Arborvitae, *Thuja orientalis*, a small tree from China with twenty or more landscape forms in extensive use in garden planting. Cones are erect, the plump seeds wingless.

Page 92. Monterey Cypress, *Cupressus macrocarpa*, formerly found naturally in a very limited area on the coast of Monterey Bay, Calif. For many years extensively cultivated for windbreaks and hedges throughout lowland Calif., but now virtually eliminated from all but central and north coastal areas by the Cypress Canker disease. It is but one of several native cypress trees which have similar rope-like twigs and globular cones of varying size. These may be listed as follows:

ADDED: Arizona Cypress, *Cupressus arizonica*, a silvery-gray, drought-resistant tree of the southwest from Calif. through Ariz. and New Mex. to W. Texas. There are rough and smooth-barked forms; a favorite ornamental in desert sections.

Modoc Cypress, *Cupressus bakeri*, a small tree found locally in N. Calif. and S. Oreg.

Gowen Cypress, *Cupressus goveniana*, includes several types sometimes classified separately found in the coast ranges from Mendocino Co. S. to Santa Barbara Co. The interesting Pygmy Cypress of the Mendocino White Plains is one of these forms.

Tecate or Forbes Cypress, *Cupressus guadalupensis*, has a limited distribution in S. Calif. and adjacent Mexico.

MacNab Cypress, *Cupressus macnabiana*, a shrubby species with fragrant foliage found at intervals in foothill areas from Sonoma and Amador Co., Calif. N. to the vicinity of Mt. Shasta.

INTRODUCED: Italian Cypress, *Cupressus sempervirens*, from the Mediterranean, has foliage and cones very similar to those of Monterey Cypress, but has a slender, pencil-like form which makes it a very popular accent tree for ornamental planting. One form has short, horizontal branches but is still columnar in form.

Page 94. Incense Cedar, *Libocedrus decurrens*, now listed as Calocedrus by some authors, distributed in mountain forest areas from S. Oreg. to S. Calif. and northern Mexico. Not found in the areas north of this. Fine-grained, fragrant wood now more highly esteemed than formerly for interior finish and for the manufacture of wooden pencils. Ornamental tree in valley and foothill plantings. In the latter use it often has a slender columnar form.

Page 97. Sierra Redwood or Big Tree, *Sequoia gigantea* (Sequoiadendron) found in scattered groves in the Calif. Sierras at 5,000 to 7,000 ft.; the most stately and massive tree on the North American continent. Short, sharp, awl-like needles and oval cones to 3 in. long with stout shield-shaped cone-scales. Grows easily from seed and young trees grow with great rapidity. Growing successfully along the coast to S. British Columbia; has great possibilities as a timber species. Becoming a popular Christmas tree in Calif. plantations.

Page 99. California Nutmeg, *Torreya californica* (Tumion), has long, sharp, bright green needles and a single-seeded fleshy, olive-like fruit borne on female trees while pollen-bearing flowers occur on male trees. Grows to good size and produces a fine-grained durable lumber, but is nowhere in dense enough stands to be commercially important. Rarely used as an ornamental.

Page 101. Western Yew, *Taxus brevifolia*, a small tree of the understory usually found in shaded situations. Foliage resembles that of coast redwood, but is light green instead of white beneath. Its single-seeded, waxy, succulent berries are an attractive feature of female trees. The brownish, fine-grained wood of yews has been noted for its use for archery bows.

INTRODUCED: English Yew, *Taxus baccata* from Europe, has dense, dark green foliage and many horticultural varieties; a common garden tree.

Japanese Yew, *Taxus cuspidata* from Japan with dwarf and other horti-cultural forms is also in ornamental use.

Page 103. The Junipers—genus *Juniperus* have male and female flowers on different trees, so that the bluish or reddish berry-like fruits are borne only on female trees. In youth the foliage is arranged in whorls of three with blue-green, spreading and pointed leaves. Older foliage is rope-like and resembles that of the cypresses. Several forms of prostrate or low-growing junipers are commonly used in ornamental plantings as ground-cover plants. These often retain the juvenile foliage, and some of the best types are from China.

Page 104. Western Juniper, *Juniperus occidentalis*, a high mountain tree which reaches great age and has an extensive range from Calif. where it is called Sierra Juniper, N. to Wash., Idaho and Mont. Old trees usually have a misshapen form due to severe climatic conditions under which they grow.

Page 106. One-Seed Juniper, *Juniperus monosperma* has a very wide range in the Rocky Mountain country from Colo. to S.E. Ariz. and E. to W. Texas, but does not occur in Calif. Its large reddish berries contain a single hard seed.

ADDED: Rocky Mountain Juniper, *Juniperus scopulorum* found throughout the interior mountain areas from Mont. and S.W. Alberta and S.E. British Columbia and E. Wash. to Nev., Ariz., New Mex. and W. Texas Not found in Calif.

Utah Juniper, *Juniperus osteosperma*, ranges throughout the Great Basin country from S.W. Wyo. and S. Mont. to S.E. Calif., Cent. Ariz. and W. New Mex.

California or Desert Juniper, *Juniperus californica*, inhabits dry areas from S. Oreg. to northern Mexico; most conspicuous in the Mojave Desert area. Short, rounded crown and reddish berries.

Alligator Juniper, *Juniperus deppeana* (pachyphloea), the tree with alligator skin bark pattern so conspicuous a part of the vegetation around the Grand Canyon in Ariz. Found also in W. Texas, New Mex., and into northern Mexico.

Other junipers in extensive use as ornamentals include various forms of the following: *J. communis, J. chinensis, J. horizontalis, J. sabina, J. squamata, J. procumbens, J. excelsa, J. virginiana* and selected landscape forms of several of the above native species.

Page 108. "Part II. The Broadleaf or Hardwood Trees." Broadleaf trees belong botanically to the Angiosperms, which have complex and often showy flowers with seeds ripening in an enclosed ovary. Usually the flower is made up of a central ovary containing ovules, a ring of stamens topped by anthers producing pollen, a circle of petals in 3's, 4's or 5's and a basal ring of more or less leaf-like sepals. However, one or more of these parts may be missing or variously modified. Some trees have male and female elements in separate flowers on the same tree (oaks and walnuts), while some species have male and female flowers on different trees and are said to be dioecious (ashes, willows and cottonwoods). Most North American hardwood trees lose their leaves in autumn and are said to be deciduous, but as one goes into the milder climatic zone along the Pacific Coast and then travels from north to south, more and more trees retain their leaves throughout the year and are said to be evergreen. Thus in tropical climates nearly all of the broadleaf trees are evergreen.

This manual groups the hardwood trees into three divisions: (1) Leaves made up of leaflets (a) arranged along a central stem (pinnate) ((b) joined at a central point (palmate). (2) Leaves with blades that are lobed in various ways. (3) Leaves simple (a) with toothed margins, (b) with entire margins.

It should be noted here that the arrangement of leaves on the twigs may be either opposite (Maples, Dogwoods, Elders, Buckeyes, Ashes) or alternate (Walnuts, Oaks, Sycamores, Birches, Cherries, etc.).

While broadleaf trees in the west are of far less commercial value than are the conifers, they still give character to much of the landscape, and they out-number the conifers in variety of species. Many species have been introduced from other parts of the world, and the complexity increases from mountain to valley areas and is greatest in relatively frostless areas of Southern California from Santa Barbara south. In a book of limited size it is not possible even to mention most of the many exotic trees which have been brought from other areas. It seems desirable to list some species which are not mentioned in the manual, but these will be kept to a minimum.

Page 110. Arizona Walnut, *Juglans major* (rupestris), a spreading tree of moderate size found along canyon bottoms from Cent. Ariz. to W. Texas and S. into northern Mexico. Does not extend into Calif. It has a large nut with sculptured shell.

ADDED: Little Walnut, *Juglans microcarpa*, with smaller fruits found from W. Texas and S. E. New Mex. S. into northern Mexico.

California Walnut, *Juglans californica* is now used to designate the shrubby and spreading walnut of coastal S. Calif. from Santa Barbara to Orange Co. Its low branching form is usually unsuitable for lumber, but it has produced some very fine burls at and below ground-level for carving and veneer. Used as a root stock and in some ornamental planting but usually supplanted by the following:

ADDED: Hinds Walnut, *Juglans hindsii*, a taller and much finer tree which occurred naturally in just two lowland areas near Walnut Creek, Contra Costa Co. and near Walnut Grove in the Sacramento Valley. In extensive use as a highway, street and ornamental tree; the species most commonly used as root stock on which the scions of English Walnut, *Juglans regia* are grown in extensive orchards for the commercial production of the edible fruits known as "English Walnut." When crossed with Engish Walnut produces a fast growing hybrid with valuable figure wood known as "Paradox" or "Claro" Walnut. When crossed with American Walnut, *J. nigra*, the Royal Hybrid results. It also often grows to large size and produces figured wood of high quality.

Trees of American Black Walnut, *J. nigra*, are occasionally planted on good soil as shade trees and English Walnut, *J. regia* is often grown in gardens and along streets as well as in orchards.

Page 115. Oregon Ash, *Fraxinus latifolia* (oregona) has opposite, compound leaves and clustered canoe-paddle-like fruits on female trees. Occurs along streams and lowlands from Cent. Calif. N. to W. Wash. In the fall the gold color of its foliage rivals that of the associated Broadleaf Maple.

ADDED: Arizona or Velvet Ash, *Fraxinus velutina*, a drought-hardy tree found at intervals throughout the southwest from S. Calif. to W. Texas and in adjacent Mexico. Twigs and leaflets coated with velvety hairs. Extensively used in highway and street planting until the past few years when the following smooth-leaved variety has become popular:

Modesto Ash, *F. velutina 'Modesto'*, a male clon with shiny leaves and good form which grows rapidly to moderate size; present in ornamental plantings throughout coastal and valley areas in Calif.

Foothill or Two-petal Ash, *Fraxinus dipetala*, a small and often shrubby tree found in foothill chaparral areas from Cent. Calif. S. to northern Mexico. Attractive cream-colored flower clusters on both male and female trees in spring cause it to be referred to as "flowering ash."

Singe-leaf Ash, *Fraxinus anomala* from W. Colo., S. Utah, S. Nev. and S.E. Calif. is another small tree with simple leaves in a genus in which all other species have compound leaves.

INTRODUCED: Green Ash, *F. Pennsylvanica* from the eastern U.S.

European Ash, *F. excelsior*, a handsome large tree; twigs with black buds.

Flowering Ash, *F. ornus* from S. Europe and W. Asia; fragrant flowers.

Evergeen Ash, *F. uhdei* from Mexico; evergreen in mild climates.

Page 117. Blueberry Elder, *Sambucus glauca*, one of several western elders distinguished by flat clusters of tiny white flowers which ripen as drooping clusters of succulent berries. Twigs have very large pith.

ADDED: Blackbead Elder, *S. melanocarpa*, shrubby, rarely a small tree.

Pacific Red Elder, *S. callicarpa*, with attractive red fruits.

Mexican Elder, *S. mexicana*, W. Texas, Ariz., to S. Calif. and Mexico.

Page 119. Black Locust, *Robinia pseudoacacia*, the hardy tree of the bean family which has been naturalized in various parts of the west since pioneer days. An attractive street tree admired for its clusters of white fragrant flowers, sturdy trunk and dense, very durable wood. There are a number of horticultural forms including:

Pink Flowering Locust, *R. pseudoacacia var. decaisneana* with pink blooms.

Thornless Locust, *R. pseudoacacia var. inermis*, without the usual thorny branchlets.

ADDED: New Mexican Locust, *Robinia neomexicana*, a tree of the southwest found from S. Colo. and Utah, S.E. Nev. and Ariz. to W. Texas and Mexico.

Page 122. The Mesquites are pod-bearing trees of southwest deserts. Screwbean Mesquite, *Prosopis pubescens* (odorata), has tightly curled pods. Distributed from W. Texas to S.E. Calif. and northern Mexico.

Page 124. Common Mesquite, *Prosopis juliflora*, has plump pods constricted between the seeds. Has extended range in South America as well as in southwestern desert areas where the following varieties are found:

Honey Mesquite, *P. j. glandulosa*, S.W. Colo., E. and S. New Mexico and S. Texas.

Western Honey Mesquite, *P. j. torreyana*, usually a shrubby small tree. Found from W. Texas through S. New Mexico, W. Ariz., S.W. Utah, S. Nev. and S. Calif.

Velvet Mesquite, *P. j. velutina* with velvety foliage, twigs and pods. Found in S.W. New Mexico, Cent. and S. Ariz. and northern Mexico.

ADDED: The Palo Verde Trees are two desert species with green stems, finely compound leaves and plump pods with slight constrictions. Both bear yellow pea-like flowers and twigs armed with spines.

Blue Paloverde, *Cercidium floridum*, flowers profusely, and bears heavy crops of pods which make good feed for stock. Found from S.E. Calif. to Cent. and S. Ariz. and S. in Mexico.

Jerusalem Thorn, *Parkinsonia aculeata*, has long compound leaves with very tiny leaflets, but is leafless during much of the hot weather. Wide range in S. Texas and S.W. Ariz, but planted as an ornamental in desert areas and has escaped in Calif. and elsewhere. Also found in Mexico and south.

Page 126. Before leaving the trees with pinnate compound leaves there should be added one with very extensive distribution throughout the west, with several races, all very similar, which are sometimes classed as varieties. It belongs to the maple genus and is often called Ash-leaved Maple.

Boxelder, *Acer negundo*, occurs along streams and lowlands in most of the western states where it is sometimes mistaken for an ash because of the compound, opposite leaves, but female trees bear clusters of winged fruits in pairs like the rest of the maples. There is a form with variegated leaves sometimes used as an ornamental.

California Buckeye, *Aesculus californica*, usually a much-branched, round-headed tree of foothill areas in Calif. where its long spikes of creamy white flowers make a fine display in springtime. Drops its leaves early and matures the large fruits after they fall.

INTRODUCED: Common Horsechestnut, *Aesculus hippocastanum* from the

Balkan peninsula, occasionally planted as a street and ornamental tree, but now not as favored as the following:

Red Horsechestnut, *Aesculus X carnea*, which has spikes of attractive red flowers. A hybrid between Common Horsechestnut and *Aesculus pavia* from the S. Atlantic coast of the U.S.

Page 129. Broadleaf, Bigleaf or Oregon Maple, *Acer macrophyllum* has very large leaves, opposite in arrangement on stout green twigs with terminal buds. Widely distributed from B.C. to S. Calif.

ADDED: Vine Maple, *Acer circinatum*, a small tree of mountain canyons and rock-slide areas from B.C. to N. Calif. Graceful 7-lobed leaves; occasionally planted as a garden ornamental.

Rocky Mountain Maple, *Acer glabrum*, a streamside tree of small size with range from Wyo., Utah, Nev., S.W. Oreg. to S. Calif., Ariz., and New Mex.

INTRODUCED: Several other maples are commonly used as ornamentals.

ADDED: Bigtooth Maple, *Acer grandidentatum* has a wide range in the interior country from Wyo. S. to W. Texas and into Mexico, but is not found in the three Pacific Coast states. It has leaves of moderate size with heavy teeth on the margins.

INTRODUCED: Other maples in common use as ornamentals include: Silver Maple, *A. saccharinum*, Red Maple, *A. rubrum*, Norway Maple, *A. platanoides*, Sycamore Maple, *A. pseudoplatanus*, and Japanese Maple, *A. palmatum*.

Page 132. The Oaks are a very numerous group of trees which have male and female flowers occurring on the same tree and acorn fruits either maturing the first or second autumn. White oaks have more or less deeply lobed leaves without spiny tips on the lobes, and acorns which usually ripen the first year. Black oaks have spiny tips on the lobes and usually two year acorns. Live Oaks have more or less holly-like leaves with at least some green leaves on the tree year round, though the Coast Live Oak loses much of its foliage in spring as the new leaves are unfolding. Tanbark Oak has evergreen foliage and acorn fruits, but is no longer classified as an oak.

Pages 133-137. White Oaks. Gambel Oak, *Quercus gambellii*, found in the Rockies from Wyo. to Mexico.

Oregon White or Post Oak, *Quercus garreyana*, the most northerly of all western oaks, from S.W. British Columbia to Cent. Calif.

Valley Oak or California White Oak, *Quercus lobata*, Calif. valleys and foothills to San Fernando Valley.

Page 139. Blue Oak, *Quercus douglasii*, Calif. foothills and lower slopes.

ADDED: Arizona White Oak, *Quercus arizonica*, W. Texas, S. New Mex., Ariz. and S. in Mexico.

Burr Oak, *Quercus macrocarpa*, though really an eastern oak, comes into N.E. Wyo., Cent. Neb. and Cent. Texas, and is quite common in cultivation as an ornamental in western states.

INTRODUCED: English Oak, *Quercus robur*, a stately shade tree from Europe. Turkey Oak, *Quercus cerris*, from S. Europe and W. Asia.

Pages 141 and 150. Black Oaks. California Black Oak, *Quercus kelloggii*, coast ranges and mountain timber belt from S. Oreg. to S. Calif.

Emory Oak, *Quercus emoryi*, W. Texas, S.W. New Mex. and Cent. Ariz.

INTRODUCED: Red Oak, *Q. rubra*, Pin Oak, *Q. palustris*, Scarlet Oak, *Q. coccinea*.

Pages 144-148. Live Oaks with green foliage during all or most of the year. Interior or Highland Live Oak, *Quercus wislizenii*, Calif. upper foothills.

Canyon Live Oak, *Quercus chrysolepis*, S.W. Oreg. through Calif.

Coast Live Oak, *Quercus agrifolia*, coast ranges, N. Calif. to Mexico.

ADDED: California Scrub Oak, *Quercus dumosa*, Calif. foothills.

Engelmann or Mesa Oak, *Quercus engelmannii*, S. Calif.

Shrub Live Oak, *Quercus turbinella*, S. Colo., S. Utah, Ariz. to W. Texas.

Oracle Oak, *Quercus moreha*, a hybrid California Black X Interior Live Oak.

INTRODUCED: Cork Oak, *Q. suber* from Spain, Holm or Holly Oak, *Q. ilex*, S. Europe.

Page 152. Tanoak or Tanbark Oak, *Lithocarpus densiflorus*, now classified in a separate genus intermediate between the oaks and chestnuts. Male flowers on long, rather stiff spikes similar to those of chestnut, with female flowers at the base. Leaves have toothed margins like those of chestnut, but the fruit is an acorn in a fringed cup. Its dense and strong wood is used for flooring in freight cars where it gives excellent service in resisting wear. Evergreen.

Page 154. The Sycamores, streamside trees of striking appearance; smooth, mottled bark, broad, palmately lobed leaves and ball-like multiple fruits. Conical buds completely enclosed by the expanded base of the leaf stem. The native species are similar.

Page 155. Arizona Sycamore, *Platanus wrightii*, S.E. and Cent. Ariz., E. New Mex. and northern Mexico. Local in S.E. Calif.

Page 157. California Sycamore, *Platanus racemosa*, valley and foothill streams from Cent. to S. Calif. and northern Mexico. In recent years subject to loss of early foliage by sycamore canker disease.

ADDED: London Plane, *Platanus X acerifolia*, a hybrid between the American Sycamore, *P. occidentalis* and Oriental Plane, *P. orientalis*. Has broad, shallowly-lobed and quite "maple-like" leaves; in very common use throughout the west as a street and ornamental tree. Somewhat more resistant to the canker disease.

Page 159. The Birches are graceful trees with thin, doubly serrate (sometimes deeply cut) leaves, bark with prominent lenticels and pendant multiple fruits like little cones. Some are favorite ornamentals with a number of horticultural forms.

Water Birch, *Betula occidentalis*, a streamside tree with wide distribution from southern B.C., Sask., and Man. to Cent. Calif. Mts.; also S. Nev., N.E. Ariz. and N.W. New Mex. Because of its smooth, golden brown bark it is called the "golden Birch."

ADDED: Western Paper Birch, *Betula papyrifera var. commutata*, a western variety of the beautiful white-barked birch of N.E. North America. Found from S.E. Alaska S. through B.C. to Wash., N. Idaho and to Cent. Nev.

Northwestern Paper Birch, *Betula papyrifera var. subcordata*, found from W. Mont., N. Idaho, N.E. Oreg. and E. Wash. N. in Canada.

INTRODUCED: European White Birch, *Betula verrucosa* (alba) has white bark and gracefully pendant branches. Several horticultural varieties; a favorite garden ornamental tree throughout the west. Paper Birch and Japanese White Birch are occasionally cultivated.

Page 161. The Alders are also streamside and bottom-land trees with smooth, gray, mottled stems, doubly serrate leaves and multiple fruits which resemble cones.

Red Alder, *Alnus rubra*, now occupies thousands of acres of cut-over lands in the Pacific Northwest where it has grown following logging and fires. Utilized for furniture and pulp. Leaves more deeply toothed than those of the following, with distinctly rolled margins.

Page 164. White Alder, *Alnus rhombifolis*, occupies the banks of mountain streams inland from B.C. through the Cascades and Sierra to northern Mexico. Finely toothed oval leaves; edges not rolled. Achieving popularity as an ornamental tree on irrigated lawns.

ADDED: Two shrubby alders with high mountain distribution are:

Sitka Alder, *Alnus sinuata*, with wavy-margined leaves, found from W. Alaska S. to Cent. Calif.

Thinleaf Alder, *Alnus tenuifolia*, has a similar northern range but continues in high mountain areas from Cent. Calif. and W. Nev. to E. Ariz. and N. New Mex.

INTRODUCED: The following alders are in cultivation as ornamentals:

Black Alder, *A. glutinosa*, European Alder, *A. cordata*, Green Alder, *A. viridis*, Japanese Alder, *A. japonica*.

Page 166. The Cherries, genus *Prunus*, includes besides deciduous and evergreen cherries, fruit and ornamental Plums, Peaches, Apricots, Almonds and Nectarines. Many are outstanding ornamentals, with some classified as Cherry Laurels as noted.

Holly-leaf Cherry or Islay, *Prunus ilicifolia*, a small tree with shiny, holly-like, broad evergreen leaves found from Cent. Calif. S. to northern Mexico in coastal and foothill areas. Frequently used as a hedge and garden shrub.

ADDED: Catalina Cherry, *Prunus lyoni*, a very similar tree from the Santa Barbara Channel Islands with larger and less spiny leaves and also larger fruits. Hybrids between these two species now in cultivation.

INTRODUCED: Other evergreen cherries or cherry-laurels:

Cherry Laurel or English Laurel, *Prunus laurocerasus*, a small tree or large shrub from S.E. Europe with large, shiny, serrate leaves and small clustered fruits. Several varieties commonly used as hedges and garden ornamentals.

Portugal Laurel, *Prunus lusitanica* from the Mediterranean has smaller, darker green and less shiny leaves and a fine display of tiny flowers on erect spikes which ripen as small black single-seeded cherries.

Page 169. Bitter Cherry, *Prunus emarginata*, a small tree with extensive distribution from W. Mont. to B.C. and S. to S. Calif., Nev., Ariz. and S.W. New Mex. Its small deciduous leaves with finely serrate margins are wedge shaped at the base with short leaf stalks.

ADDED: Western Choke Cherry, *Prunus virginiana* (demissa) has a continent-wide range from Newfoundland to B.C. S. to Ga. on the east and to W. Calif. in the west. Forms dense thickets in much of the mountain country. Oval leaves with finely serrate margins tapered to the tip; the red fruits ⅓ in. in diameter.

Klamath Plum, *Prunus subcordata* has rounded, sometimes nearly heart-shaped leaves; found from S. Oreg. to Cent. Calif.

Desert Apricot, *Prunus fremontii* has a limited range in S. Calif. and northern Mexico.

INTRODUCED: Among many ornamentals from around the world may be mentioned:

Myrobalan Plum, *Prunus ceracifera*, a root-stock from S.W. Asia.

Japanese Flowering Cherries, *P. serrulata* and others.

Garden Plum, *P. domestica*, from Eurasia.

These and others have escaped from cultivation in several places in the west.

Page 171. Golden Chinkapin, *Castanopsis chrysophylla*, an attractive evergreen tree found from W. Wash. S. to Cent. Calif. in the coast ranges and occasionally in the Sierra where a shrub form grows in dense stands at higher elev. The narrow, deep green, leathery leaves taper to the tip and short stem. They have entire margins and are gold colored beneath. The wood has an attractive figure, but is very difficult to season.

Page 173. The Poplars, genus *Populus*, in the same family with willows from which they differ in having broader, rounded leaves on long and often flattened leaf stalks, buds with many scales and generally larger size. Both are dioecious with worldwide distribution in the northern hemisphere; both grow easily from cuttings.

Aspen, Quaking Aspen, *Populus tremuloides* has nearly continental distribution, but in the west is usually a tree of high mts. Spreads in natural stands by root sprouts, but not easily grown in cultivation at lower elev. Named from the trembling leaves.

Page 176. Black Cottonwood, *Populus trichocarpa*, the largest of the western poplars with wide distribution from B.C., S. along the coast ranges to S. Calif. and at higher elev. along streams in the Sierra. Its large leaves with serrate margins taper to a slender point; dark green above and yellowish beneath. In the Pacific Northwest where it reaches large size it is sawed into rough lumber and logs are shipped to Japan for manufacture there. As with other poplars it is of increasing interest for pulp and paper products.

Page 178. Fremont Cottonwood, *Populus fremontii*, also known as Valley Cottonwood, is found in valleys from N. Calif. S. to northern Mexico and from S.W. Utah and Nev. along desert streams to Ariz. and New Mex. Its ease of cultivation, rapid growth and broad, rounded crown give it definite landscape value in interior irrigated districts, but it is not a commercial species. A variety *wislizenii* is found in the W. Rockies and S. to northern Mexico.

ADDED: Plains Cottonwood, *Populus sargentii*, found along the E. side of the Rocky Mts. from Mont., Wyo., E. Colo., to N.E. New Mex. and N.W. Texas and farther E. on the plains.

INTRODUCED: A number of cottonwoods from around the world are common in cultivation and a number of natural hybrids and crosses are being tested for hardiness and rapidity of growth. Some of the more common are:

Silver Poplar, *Populus alba* and *var. bolleana* from Europe, with silvery, maple-shaped leaves and smooth, gray-green trunks.

Lombardy Poplar, *Populus nigra italica*, a male clon from Italy with tall, slender habit of growth, making it a popular ornamental.

Common Cottonwood, *Populus deltoides*, from E. North America which has become established in various western situations.

Balsam Poplar, *Populus balsamifera*, a northern species with resinous, fragrant smelling buds. Local in Wyo., Idaho and Colo.; has been planted as a windbreak tree in Oreg.

Page 180. The Willows, genus *Salix* are a numerous company of small to medium-sized trees distributed from extreme northern areas around the northern hemisphere, usually along streams and in moist places. They usually have long, narrow leaves tapering to a slender point with finely toothed margins and short leaf stalks which often have a pair of leafy stipules at the base. The twigs are smooth and the buds are enclosed by a single bud scale. They propagate easily from cuttings and grow rapidly, but are short lived. Male and female flowers occur on separate trees (dioecious) and the cottony winged seeds quickly lose their germinative capacity. Few willows become large enough to produce lumber, but some are important in the making of wicker furniture, and many have been used in the stabilization of stream banks and levees. A few are in common use as ornamentals.

Twenty willows are native in the western states of which only one was selected for presentation in this text:

Pacific Willow, *Salix lasiandra*, a tree of moderate size to 45 ft. also known as Yellow Willow and Black Willow. The largest of the native willows with the longest and broadest leaves, to 6 in. long by 1¼ in. broad. Grows along stream banks from Puget Sound to S. Calif. at increasing elev. in the mts.

The other western willows are too numerous for inclusion here, but their names and ranges will be found in the *Check List of Forest Trees of the U.S.* They are really not as well known as the following ornamental willows:

INTRODUCED: Weeping Willow, *Salix babylonica* from China grows to 70 ft. with a broadly rounded crown of pendant branches. A familiar tree ·in cultivation throughout much of the U.S.

Ringleaf Weeping Willow, *Salix babylonica var. crispa,* has narrower and more blue-green leaves which are twisted in rings around the twigs.

Golden Weeping Willow, *Salix alba*, a similar but smaller tree with golden yellow twigs, known as type "Tristis."

Pekin or Corkscrew Willow, *Salix matsudana "tortuosa,"* another Chinese tree with drooping branches and contorted leaves.

Basket Willow, *Salix viminalis* from Eurasia, grown in local areas for basketry and has sometimes escaped into the neighborhood.

Pussy Willow, *Salix discolor*, a small ornamental tree of wide distribution reaching into the Pacific Northwest. Cultivated as a garden ornamental for the "pussy-like" flower buds in spring.

Japanese Pussy Willow, *Salix purpurea var. multinervis*, a garden ornamental in Calif. and parts of the west.

Note: The tree called Desert Willow, *Chilopsis linearis* belongs to the

Bignonia family and has showy flowers (see p. 185).

Page 183. Hackberries, genus *Celtis*, hardy trees belonging to the Elm family, with broad leaves tapering to a slender point from a short leaf-stalk, and more or less serrate margins; the fruits are small, hard berries.

Western Hackberry, *Celtis reticulata*, also called Palo Blanco or Netleaf Hackberry, grows to 30 ft.; native from Wyo., Idaho and W. Wash. to S. Calif. and E. through Ariz. and New Mex. to W. Texas. Though hardy it is rarely cultivated for ornament.

INTRODUCED: Hackberry, *Celtis occidentalis*, a larger tree quite widely distributed in the eastern and southern U.S. Occasionally cultivated as a shade tree.

European Hackberry, *Celtis australis*, a handsome tree growing to 80 ft. with trunk marked by warty excrescences and a broad spreading crown. A good street tree; hardy in valley areas with irrigation. Native in S. Europe, W. Asia and N. Africa.

Chinese Hackberry, *Celtis sinensis* from China and Japan, grows to a sturdy tree 60 ft. tall and does well in Calif. interior valleys.

Page 184. The Elms, genus *Ulmus*, are in the same family as the Hackberries and trees of the two genera resemble each other quite closely. No elms are native in the western states, but some species have been planted since pioneer days as street, park and shade trees and some have reached large size. The elms have broadly rounded leaves with doubly serrate margins, a more or less heart-shaped base and are often rough to touch. So far the Dutch Elm Disease and Phloem Necrosis are not present in the west, but Elm Leaf Beetle is a serious defoliator of elms unless controlled by spraying. The chief elms in cultivation are:

INTRODUCED: American Elm, *Ulmus americana* from the eastern U.S. forest region.

English Elm, *Ulmus procera* from Europe.

Scotch Elm or Wych Elm, *Ulmus glabra* from Europe.

Camperdown Elm, *Ulmus glabra* "*camperdownii*," a weeping garden specimen.

Siberian Elm, *Ulmus pumila* from Asia extensively planted for windbreaks and shelter throughout dry sections of the west.

Chinese Elm, *Ulmus parvifolia*, a small-leaved species which bears fruit in the fall and is evergreen in mild coastal areas.

INTRODUCED: Sawleaf Elm, *Zelkova zelkova* or Keaki from Japan, another Elm family tree which grows to 100 ft.; a hardy and pest-free ornamental tree used in parks, streets and gardens. Lance-like leaves rounded at the base and tapered to the tip with saw-like teeth above the middle. Fruit is a small berry-like drupe with a single seed.

Page 185. Broadleaf trees with entire margined leaves.

A number of additional trees could be added to the seven genera described under this heading, especially among ornamental trees. Many of the Acacias in which the leaves are reduced to broadened leaf-stems (Phyllodea) would come under this designation. Others would be: Hakea, Magnolias, Cinnamomum, Persea and Pittosporum.

Desert Willow, *Chilopsis linearis*, a desert tree with long and very narrow leaves, showy lavender flowers and long, slender seed pods resembling those of Catalpa which is in the same family. Though a hardy and handsome small tree it is rarely cultivated.

Page 187. The Mountain Mahoganies, genus *Cercocarpus*, are small to medium-sized trees with small leaves, very hard wood which results in the local name "hardtack" and single-seeded fruits fitted with a long, feathery appendage. Some have leaves serrate above the middle.

Curlleaf Cercocarpus or Mountain Mahogany, *Cercocarpus ledifolius*, a mountain species of dry slopes found from Wash. and Mont. S. through E. Oreg. to S.E. Calif. and easterly in Nev., Utah, W. Colo. and N. Ariz. Leathery leaves 1 in. by ¼ in. wide with rolled margins. Rarely grows to more than 25 ft. tall.

ADDED: Birchleaf Cercocarpus, *Cercocarpus betuloides* with leaves serrate above the middle resembling those of birch. Found in chaparral areas from W. Oreg. S. in Sierra and coast ranges to northern Mexico and also in Cent. Ariz. *Var. macrourus* is in S.W. Oreg. and N.W. Calif. and *var. blanchae* and *var. traskae* are found only on the Santa Barbara Channel Islands.

Hairy Cercocarpus, *Cercocarpus breviflorus*, native in W. Texas, Ariz., New Mex. and W. in northern Mexico.

Page 189. The Gums, genus *Eucalyptus*, a very complex genus of trees from Australia, containing more than 500 species and a number of varieties and hybrids. The first seeds were brought to Calif. on clipper ships in the middle 1850's and they have ever since been a major feature of the coastal and valley landscape. At one time about 50,000 acres were planted to Eucalyptus, chiefly of the three species listed here, but some died from frost, others from poor soil and drought, and those on good land were usually removed after a time for the growing of more valuable irrigated crops when sufficient water became available.

The University of Calif. for a number of years carried on test planting of many promising species at the Santa Monica and Chico Forestry Stations

Appendix

and issued bulletins on growth and development. Some were found to be most useful for windbreaks to protect citrus and other crops from wind damage. Others are being used for pulp and paper products; still others for highway beautification, soil stabilization and as garden ornamentals. The search continues and now more than 100 species are being tested.

Page 190. Blue Gum, *Eucalyptus globulus*, fastest growing in Calif. and at present the premier windbreak tree. The chief species in nearly 2,000 miles of windbreaks protecting crops in S. Calif. and a major feature of the coastal landscape from Los Angeles to Eureka.

Page 193. Red Gum, *Eucalyptus camaldulensis* (rostrata), slower growing but somewhat more drought and frost hardy than Blue Gum; one of the best for inland valley planting. Closely resembles Forest Red Gum, *Euc. tereticornis*, and Moitch or Desert Gum, *Euc. rudis* which are often planted with it; there are probably hybrids between these.

Page 196. Sugar Gum, *Eucalyptus cladocalyx* (corynocalyx), a tall, stately and drought-resistant tree which does best in S. Calif.; not as frost hardy as the above species. A good ornamental tree in mild but dry coastal areas.

ADDED: Manna Gum, *Eucalyptus viminalis* has proved frost resistant in the upper Sacramento Valley and along the coast N. of San Francisco. Now being experimentally planted on areas of cut-over redwood land in Mendocino Co. for possible manufacture of particle-board. Beautiful ornamental with creamy white trunk and ribbony foliage.

Red Ironbark, *Eucalyptus sideroxylon*, one of the best for highway planting in interior valleys; frost hardy and very drought resistant. Blue-green foliage, coal black bark and attractive clusters of pink flowers in 3's and 5's.

Scarlet Gum, *Eucalyptus ficifolia* has fig-like, deep green, broad leaves and masses of large scarlet flowers which nearly cover the tree at blooming time. These ripen as heavy pods the size and shape of smoking pipe bowls, and contain large winged seeds. Not frost hardy away from the coast but a striking ornamental from the San Francisco Bay area south.

Silver-leaved Mountain Gum, *Eucalyptus pulverulenta* has round, silvery gray foliage; one of the most frost hardy ornamentals.

Red Box, *Eucalyptus polyanthemos* has round or oval leaves of gray-green about the size of silver dollars and terminal clusters of tiny white flowers and seed pods. Good hardiness; a very satisfactory street and highway ornamental.

The large number of species now being tested will undoubtedly result in discovering other desirable ornamental species and perhaps still others which will prove to be economically valuable for their wood.

Page 198. The Buckthorns, genus *Rhamnus*, are shrubs or small trees with simple leaves, succulent, berry-like fruits, some with important medicinal qualities in the bark.

Cascara Buckthorn, *Rhamnus purshiana* ranges from N. Calif. through W. Oreg. and Wash. to S. W. British Columbia and E. to N. W. Mont. and N. W. Idaho. The bark is still a valuable product in the Pacific Northwest.

ADDED: California Buckthorn, *Rhamnus californica*, usually a shrub of chaparral slopes found from S. W. Oreg. through Calif. foothills to Mexico; a *var. ursina* ranges E. in mts. to New Mex., Cent. Ariz., S. Nev. and S. E. Calif., and occasionally reaching tree size. Several other ornamental varities are in cultivation.

Hollyleaf Buckthorn, *Rhamnus crocea* and its varieties *ilicifolia* and *pirifolia*, also shrubs and occasionally small trees with spiny, holly-like foliage and succulent red fruits. Found in chaparral areas from N. Calif. to northern Mexico and E. to N. W. Ariz.

INTRODUCED: Italian Buckthorn, *Rhamnus alaternus* and its *var. variegata*, occasionally used in ornamental plantings in Calif.

Page 200. The Dogwoods, genus *Cornus*, have simple, opposite leaves with clustered small flowers in some species subtended by showy bracts, fine-grained, white wood of high quality and foliage which turns attractive color in fall.

Pacific Dogwood, *Cornus nuttallii*, a tree found in forest understory from S. W. British Columbia through W. Wash. and Oreg. to S. Calif. in mts. and locally in N. Idaho. It flowers just before the leaves open and in the Puget Sound country has a second flowering period in late summer. Very ornamental species but needs some shade and care to do well in gardens.

ADDED: Western Dogwood, *Cornus occidentalis*, usually a shrub with narrower leaves and less showy flowers than the above; there is a hybrid form within the range, apparently a cross with Red Osier Dogwood, *Cornus stolonifera* which has been called California Dogwood, *Cornus X californica*.

Blackfruit Dogwood, *Cornus sessilis*, a shrub or small tree to 13 ft. of the foothills of N. Calif. Sierra and coast mts.

INTRODUCED: Evergreen Dogwood, *Cornus capitata*, an evergreen species from the Himalayas with 4 in. leaves which taper both to tip and stem, narrow white bracts below the flower cluster and multiple fruits about 1 in. in diameter. Occasionally cultivated in mild areas.

Page 203. California Laurel, *Umbellularia californica*, also known as Bay, Pepperwood and Oregon Myrtle. Its leaves when crushed have a strong, spicy odor which distinguishes it from all other western trees. Its heavy, fine-grained and figured wood is used in the manufacture of turned articles and makes a very beautiful veneer. Found from S. W. Oreg. through the coast ranges to S. Calif. and in the Sierra at intervals to Tulare Co. On bottomlands it grows to a large tree, but becomes misshapen when exposed to ocean winds.

INTRODUCED: Grecian Laurel, *Laurus nobilis* from the Mediterranean has leaves which are more tapered both to tip and stem and are darker green. These have a somewhat similar fragrance when crushed and are used in cooking. Spreads easily by root sprouts and makes attractive clumps in ornamental plantings. Fruits are smaller.

Page 205. The Madrones, genus *Arbutus*, heath family trees and shrubs with evergreen leaves, tiny white, bell-like flowers in clusters and succulent orange or red berry-like fruits. Native in the Mediterranean as well as in the western and southwestern U. S.

Pacific Madrone, *Arbutus menziesii*, a large tree of spectacular beauty found from Cent. Calif. through the coast ranges to S. W. British Columbia and occasionally in the Sierra Nevada, and in smaller form in S. Calif. The outer bark of branches scales off, leaving the trunk smooth and mottled in red and tan colors. The wood is fine-grained, hard and with a pleasing figure, but not easily seasoned. Not called laurel, but in the northern area known as Arbutus. Recently trees in Cent. Calif. have been attacked by a leaf-spot disease which has killed trees here and there, but this may be due in part to weakened condition after several dry years.

Page 208. Texas Madrone, *Arbutus texana*, found in a rather limited area in W. Texas, S. E. New Mex. and adjacent Mexico. Not called Manzanita as this term is properly applied to another genus of shrubs, also in the heath family—Arctostaphylos. Widely distributed in the chaparral areas of Calif., but much branched, rarely reaching tree size.

Arizona Madrone, *Arbutus arizonica*, a very similar species found in S. Ariz., S. W. New Mex. and adjacent Mexico. Both of these southwestern Madrones are very similar to a Madrone found in Mexico, *Arbutus xalapensis*, and were formerly classified as varieties.

INTRODUCED: Strawberry Tree, *Arbutus unedo* from the Mediterranean region, quite commonly used as an ornamental in coastal areas of Calif. Its leaves have serrate margins and quite closely resemble those of our native Toyon or Christmas Berry, *Heteromeles arbutifolia* which occurs in foothill chaparral areas and is a favorite decoration at Christmas because of its clusters of bright red berries and dark green foliage. Occasionally becomes a small tree. Strawberry Tree is so named from its clustered fruits which are about the color, size and appearance of strawberries. May grow to 25 ft., but is usually smaller and makes an excellent tall hedge.

In closing, it may be noted that among native trees not included in the text are the Hawthorns, *Crataegus* with eight species of small trees listed as within the western states; Oregon Crabapple, *Malus diversifolia*, an attractive rose family tree in the coastal area from B. C. to N. W. Calif.; and Fremontia, *Fremontia californica*, a small evergreen tree of the Calif. foothills with strikingly beautiful golden flowers.

BIBLIOGRAPHY

The following references on western trees will be helpful in giving added information. Many of them will probably be available in local libraries. Also consult your State Forester or Agricultural Extension Service for references on trees within your state.

Bailey, L. H., and Ethel Zoe Bailey, *Hortus Second*, The Macmillan Company, New York, 1947. 778 pp.

Blakely, W. F., *A Key to the Eucalypts*, 2nd ed., Forestry and Timber Bureau, Canberra, Australia, 1955. 360 pp. $3.50

Bowers, N. A., *Cone Bearing Trees of the Pacific Coast*, 7th printing, Pacific Books, Palo Alto, 1965. 164 pp., illust. $4.95

Brush, W. D., and G. H. Collingwood, *Knowing Your Trees*, American Forestry Association, Washington, D. C. 328 pp., illust. $6.00

Burlison, Guernsey and Johnson, *Trees of Idaho*, Bulletin 289, Agr. Extension Service, Univ. of Idaho, Moscow, Idaho, 1958. 24 pp., illust.

Coffman, John D., *Forests and Trees of the National Park System*, Supt. of Documents, Washington, D. C., 1955. $.15

Cunningham, G. C., *Forest Flora of Canada*, Bulletin 121, Canada Department of Northern Affairs and National Resources, Ottawa, 1959. 144 pp., illust.

Harlow, W. M., and E. S. Harrar, *Textbook of Dendrology*, 4th ed., McGraw-Hill Book Co., New York, 1958. 561 pp., illust. $8.50

Hayes, D. W., and Geo. A. Garrison, *Key to Important Woody Plants of Eastern Oregon and Washington*, U.S.D.A. Agric. Handbook No. 148, Supt. of Documents, Washington, D. C., 1960. 227 pp. $2.00

Important Forest Trees of the U. S., U.S.D.A. Separate No. 2156, Supt. of Documents, Washington, D. C., 1950. Illust. $.20

Jepson, W. L., *Trees of California*, Univ. of Calif. Press, Berkeley. 229 pp., illust.

Kearney, T. H., and R. Peebles, etc., *Arizona Flora*, Univ. of Calif. Press, Berkeley, 1951. 1032 pp., illust. $7.50

Little, Elbert L., Jr., *Check List of Native and Naturalized Trees of the United States including Alaska*, U.S.D.A. Supt. of Documents, Washington, D. C., 1953. 400 pp. $2.00

Little, Elbert L., Jr., *Southwestern Trees*, Agricultural Handbook No. 9, U.S.D.A., Supt. of Documents, Washington, D. C. 109 pp., illust. $.30

Lyons, C. P., *Trees, Shrubs and Flowers to Know in British Columbia*, J. M. Dent and Sons Ltd., Vancouver, 1952. 168 pp., illust. $3.50

McMinn, H., and Evelyn Maino, *An Illustrated Manual of Pacific Coast Trees*, Univ. of Calif. Press, Berkeley, 1935. 409 pp., illust. Contains a number of trees introduced as ornamentals.

Maino, Evelyn, and Frances Howard, *Ornamental Trees, An Illustrated Guide to their Selection and Care*, Univ. of Calif. Press, Berkeley, 1955. 219 pp., illust. $3.75

Mathias, Mildred, and Elizabeth McClintock, *A Checklist of Woody Ornamental Plants of California*, Manual 32, Calif. Agr. Experiment Station, Univ. of Calif. Press, Berkeley, 1963. Paper. $.75

Metcalf, Woodbridge, *Native Trees of the San Francisco Bay Region*, Univ. of Calif. Press, Berkeley, 1959. 71 pp., paper, illust. $1.50

Native Trees of Canada, 4th ed., Dominion Forest Service, Canada Dept. of Mines and Resources, Ottawa, 1949. 233 pp., illust. $1.50

Peattie, Donald Culross, *A Natural History of Western Trees*, Houghton Mifflin Co., Boston, 1953. 751 pp., illust. $6.00

Pratt, Rutherford, *American Trees—A Book of Discovery*, Dodd Mead Co., New York, 1952. 266 pp., illust. $3.50

Sargent, Charles S., *Manual of Trees of North America*, 2 vol. set, Dover Publications, Inc., New York, 1965. Reprint, paper. $6.00 set.

Sudworth, George B., *Forest Trees of the Pacific Slope*, Bulletin U. S. Forest Service, Washington, D. C., 1908. Dover reprint, 1966. 441 pp., illust. $4.00.

Tilford, Paul E., Ed., *Shade Tree Evaluation*, tree lists for sections of the U. S., Bulletin of International Shade Tree Conference and Dept. of Horticulture, Ohio State University, Wooster, Ohio, 1965. 29 pp.

INDEX

A CATALOGUE OF SELECTED DOVER BOOKS
IN ALL FIELDS OF INTEREST

A CATALOGUE OF SELECTED DOVER BOOKS
IN ALL FIELDS OF INTEREST

WHAT IS SCIENCE?, *N. Campbell*
The role of experiment and measurement, the function of mathematics, the nature of scientific laws, the difference between laws and theories, the limitations of science, and many similarly provocative topics are treated clearly and without technicalities by an eminent scientist. "Still an excellent introduction to scientific philosophy," H. Margenau in *Physics Today*. "A first-rate primer . . . deserves a wide audience," *Scientific American*. 192pp. 5⅜ x 8.

60043-2 Paperbound $1.25

THE NATURE OF LIGHT AND COLOUR IN THE OPEN AIR, *M. Minnaert*
Why are shadows sometimes blue, sometimes green, or other colors depending on the light and surroundings? What causes mirages? Why do multiple suns and moons appear in the sky? Professor Minnaert explains these unusual phenomena and hundreds of others in simple, easy-to-understand terms based on optical laws and the properties of light and color. No mathematics is required but artists, scientists, students, and everyone fascinated by these "tricks" of nature will find thousands of useful and amazing pieces of information. Hundreds of observational experiments are suggested which require no special equipment. 200 illustrations; 42 photos. xvi + 362pp. 5⅜ x 8.

20196-1 Paperbound $2.75

THE STRANGE STORY OF THE QUANTUM, AN ACCOUNT FOR THE GENERAL READER OF THE GROWTH OF IDEAS UNDERLYING OUR PRESENT ATOMIC KNOWLEDGE, *B. Hoffmann*
Presents lucidly and expertly, with barest amount of mathematics, the problems and theories which led to modern quantum physics. Dr. Hoffmann begins with the closing years of the 19th century, when certain trifling discrepancies were noticed, and with illuminating analogies and examples takes you through the brilliant concepts of Planck, Einstein, Pauli, Broglie, Bohr, Schroedinger, Heisenberg, Dirac, Sommerfeld, Feynman, etc. This edition includes a new, long postscript carrying the story through 1958. "Of the books attempting an account of the history and contents of our modern atomic physics which have come to my attention, this is the best," H. Margenau, Yale University, in *American Journal of Physics*. 32 tables and line illustrations. Index. 275pp. 5⅜ x 8.

20518-5 Paperbound $2.00

GREAT IDEAS OF MODERN MATHEMATICS: THEIR NATURE AND USE, *Jagjit Singh*
Reader with only high school math will understand main mathematical ideas of modern physics, astronomy, genetics, psychology, evolution, etc. better than many who use them as tools, but comprehend little of their basic structure. Author uses his wide knowledge of non-mathematical fields in brilliant exposition of differential equations, matrices, group theory, logic, statistics, problems of mathematical foundations, imaginary numbers, vectors, etc. Original publication. 2 appendixes. 2 indexes. 65 ills. 322pp. 5⅜ x 8.

20587-8 Paperbound $2.50

THE MUSIC OF THE SPHERES: THE MATERIAL UNIVERSE — FROM ATOM TO QUASAR, SIMPLY EXPLAINED, *Guy Murchie*
Vast compendium of fact, modern concept and theory, observed and calculated data, historical background guides intelligent layman through the material universe. Brilliant exposition of earth's construction, explanations for moon's craters, atmospheric components of Venus and Mars (with data from recent fly-by's), sun spots, sequences of star birth and death, neighboring galaxies, contributions of Galileo, Tycho Brahe, Kepler, etc.; and (Vol. 2) construction of the atom (describing newly discovered sigma and xi subatomic particles), theories of sound, color and light, space and time, including relativity theory, quantum theory, wave theory, probability theory, work of Newton, Maxwell, Faraday, Einstein, de Broglie, etc. "Best presentation yet offered to the intelligent general reader," *Saturday Review*. Revised (1967). Index. 319 illustrations by the author. Total of xx + 644pp. 5⅜ x 8½.
21809-0, 21810-4   Two volume set, paperbound $5.00

FOUR LECTURES ON RELATIVITY AND SPACE, *Charles Proteus Steinmetz*
Lecture series, given by great mathematician and electrical engineer, generally considered one of the best popular-level expositions of special and general relativity theories and related questions. Steinmetz translates complex mathematical reasoning into language accessible to laymen through analogy, example and comparison. Among topics covered are relativity of motion, location, time; of mass; acceleration; 4-dimensional time-space; geometry of the gravitational field; curvature and bending of space; non-Euclidean geometry. Index. 40 illustrations. x + 142pp. 5⅜ x 8½.   61771-8 Paperbound $1.50

HOW TO KNOW THE WILD FLOWERS, *Mrs. William Starr Dana*
Classic nature book that has introduced thousands to wonders of American wild flowers. Color-season principle of organization is easy to use, even by those with no botanical training, and the genial, refreshing discussions of history, folklore, uses of over 1,000 native and escape flowers, foliage plants are informative as well as fun to read. Over 170 full-page plates, collected from several editions, may be colored in to make permanent records of finds. Revised to conform with 1950 edition of Gray's Manual of Botany. xlii + 438pp.
5⅜ x 8½.   20332-8 Paperbound $2.50

MANUAL OF THE TREES OF NORTH AMERICA, *Charles Sprague Sargent*
Still unsurpassed as most comprehensive, reliable study of North American tree characteristics, precise locations and distribution. By dean of American dendrologists. Every tree native to U.S., Canada, Alaska; 185 genera, 717 species, described in detail—leaves, flowers, fruit, winterbuds, bark, wood, growth habits, etc. plus discussion of varieties and local variants, immaturity variations. Over 100 keys, including unusual 11-page analytical key to genera, aid in identification. 783 clear illustrations of flowers, fruit, leaves. An unmatched permanent reference work for all nature lovers. Second enlarged (1926) edition. Synopsis of families. Analytical key to genera. Glossary of technical terms. Index. 783 illustrations, 1 map. Total of 982pp. 5⅜ x 8.
20277-1, 20278-X Two volume set, paperbound $6.00

IT'S FUN TO MAKE THINGS FROM SCRAP MATERIALS,
Evelyn Glantz Hershoff
What use are empty spools, tin cans, bottle tops? What can be made from rubber bands, clothes pins, paper clips, and buttons? This book provides simply worded instructions and large diagrams showing you how to make cookie cutters, toy trucks, paper turkeys, Halloween masks, telephone sets, aprons, linoleum block- and spatter prints — in all 399 projects! Many are easy enough for young children to figure out for themselves; some challenging enough to entertain adults; all are remarkably ingenious ways to make things from materials that cost pennies or less! Formerly "Scrap Fun for Everyone." Index. 214 illustrations. 373pp. 5⅜ x 8½.   21251-3 Paperbound $2.00

SYMBOLIC LOGIC and THE GAME OF LOGIC, *Lewis Carroll*
"Symbolic Logic" is not concerned with modern symbolic logic, but is instead a collection of over 380 problems posed with charm and imagination, using the syllogism and a fascinating diagrammatic method of drawing conclusions. In "The Game of Logic" Carroll's whimsical imagination devises a logical game played with 2 diagrams and counters (included) to manipulate hundreds of tricky syllogisms. The final section, "Hit or Miss" is a lagniappe of 101 additional puzzles in the delightful Carroll manner. Until this reprint edition, both of these books were rarities costing up to $15 each. Symbolic Logic: Index. xxxi + 199pp. The Game of Logic: 96pp. 2 vols. bound as one. 5⅜ x 8.
20492-8 Paperbound $2.50

MATHEMATICAL PUZZLES OF SAM LOYD, PART I
selected and edited by M. Gardner
Choice puzzles by the greatest American puzzle creator and innovator. Selected from his famous collection, "Cyclopedia of Puzzles," they retain the unique style and historical flavor of the originals. There are posers based on arithmetic, algebra, probability, game theory, route tracing, topology, counter and sliding block, operations research, geometrical dissection. Includes the famous "14-15" puzzle which was a national craze, and his "Horse of a Different Color" which sold millions of copies. 117 of his most ingenious puzzles in all. 120 line drawings and diagrams. Solutions. Selected references. xx + 167pp. 5⅜ x 8.
20498-7 Paperbound $1.35

STRING FIGURES AND HOW TO MAKE THEM, *Caroline Furness Jayne*
107 string figures plus variations selected from the best primitive and modern examples developed by Navajo, Apache, pygmies of Africa, Eskimo, in Europe, Australia, China, etc. The most readily understandable, easy-to-follow book in English on perennially popular recreation. Crystal-clear exposition; step-by-step diagrams. Everyone from kindergarten children to adults looking for unusual diversion will be endlessly amused. Index. Bibliography. Introduction by A. C. Haddon. 17 full-page plates, 960 illustrations. xxiii + 401pp. 5⅜ x 8½.
20152-X Paperbound $2.50

PAPER FOLDING FOR BEGINNERS, *W. D. Murray and F. J. Rigney*
A delightful introduction to the varied and entertaining Japanese art of origami (paper folding), with a full, crystal-clear text that anticipates every difficulty; over 275 clearly labeled diagrams of all important stages in creation. You get results at each stage, since complex figures are logically developed from simpler ones. 43 different pieces are explained: sailboats, frogs, roosters, etc. 6 photographic plates. 279 diagrams. 95pp. 5⅜ x 8⅜.
20713-7 Paperbound $1.00

PRINCIPLES OF ART HISTORY,
H. Wölfflin
Analyzing such terms as "baroque," "classic," "neoclassic," "primitive," "picturesque," and 164 different works by artists like Botticelli, van Cleve, Dürer, Hobbema, Holbein, Hals, Rembrandt, Titian, Brueghel, Vermeer, and many others, the author establishes the classifications of art history and style on a firm, concrete basis. This classic of art criticism shows what really occurred between the 14th-century primitives and the sophistication of the 18th century in terms of basic attitudes and philosophies. "A remarkable lesson in the art of seeing," *Sat. Rev. of Literature.* Translated from the 7th German edition. 150 illustrations. 254pp. 6⅛ x 9¼. 20276-3 Paperbound $2.50

PRIMITIVE ART,
Franz Boas
This authoritative and exhaustive work by a great American anthropologist covers the entire gamut of primitive art. Pottery, leatherwork, metal work, stone work, wood, basketry, are treated in detail. Theories of primitive art, historical depth in art history, technical virtuosity, unconscious levels of patterning, symbolism, styles, literature, music, dance, etc. A must book for the interested layman, the anthropologist, artist, handicrafter (hundreds of unusual motifs), and the historian. Over 900 illustrations (50 ceramic vessels, 12 totem poles, etc.). 376pp. 5⅜ x 8. 20025-6 Paperbound $2.50

THE GENTLEMAN AND CABINET MAKER'S DIRECTOR,
Thomas Chippendale
A reprint of the 1762 catalogue of furniture designs that went on to influence generations of English and Colonial and Early Republic American furniture makers. The 200 plates, most of them full-page sized, show Chippendale's designs for French (Louis XV), Gothic, and Chinese-manner chairs, sofas, canopy and dome beds, cornices, chamber organs, cabinets, shaving tables, commodes, picture frames, frets, candle stands, chimney pieces, decorations, etc. The drawings are all elegant and highly detailed; many include construction diagrams and elevations. A supplement of 24 photographs shows surviving pieces of original and Chippendale-style pieces of furniture. Brief biography of Chippendale by N. I. Bienenstock, editor of *Furniture World.* Reproduced from the 1762 edition. 200 plates, plus 19 photographic plates. vi + 249pp. 9⅛ x 12¼. 21601-2 Paperbound $4.00

AMERICAN ANTIQUE FURNITURE: A BOOK FOR AMATEURS,
Edgar G. Miller, Jr.
Standard introduction and practical guide to identification of valuable American antique furniture. 2115 illustrations, mostly photographs taken by the author in 148 private homes, are arranged in chronological order in extensive chapters on chairs, sofas, chests, desks, bedsteads, mirrors, tables, clocks, and other articles. Focus is on furniture accessible to the collector, including simpler pieces and a larger than usual coverage of Empire style. Introductory chapters identify structural elements, characteristics of various styles, how to avoid fakes, etc. "We are frequently asked to name some book on American furniture that will meet the requirements of the novice collector, the beginning dealer, and . . . the general public. . . . We believe Mr. Miller's two volumes more completely satisfy this specification than any other work," *Antiques.* Appendix. Index. Total of vi + 1106pp. 7⅞ x 10¾.
21599-7, 21600-4 Two volume set, paperbound $10.00

THE BAD CHILD'S BOOK OF BEASTS, MORE BEASTS FOR WORSE CHILDREN, and A MORAL ALPHABET, *H. Belloc*
Hardly an anthology of humorous verse has appeared in the last 50 years without at least a couple of these famous nonsense verses. But one must see the entire volumes — with all the delightful original illustrations by Sir Basil Blackwood — to appreciate fully Belloc's charming and witty verses that play so subacidly on the platitudes of life and morals that beset his day — and ours. A great humor classic. Three books in one. Total of 157pp. 5⅜ x 8.
20749-8 Paperbound $1.25

THE DEVIL'S DICTIONARY, *Ambrose Bierce*
Sardonic and irreverent barbs puncturing the pomposities and absurdities of American politics, business, religion, literature, and arts, by the country's greatest satirist in the classic tradition. Epigrammatic as Shaw, piercing as Swift, American as Mark Twain, Will Rogers, and Fred Allen, Bierce will always remain the favorite of a small coterie of enthusiasts, and of writers and speakers whom he supplies with "some of the most gorgeous witticisms of the English language" (H. L. Mencken). Over 1000 entries in alphabetical order. 144pp. 5⅜ x 8.
20487-1 Paperbound $1.25

THE COMPLETE NONSENSE OF EDWARD LEAR.
This is the only complete edition of this master of gentle madness available at a popular price. *A Book of Nonsense, Nonsense Songs, More Nonsense Songs and Stories* in their entirety with all the old favorites that have delighted children and adults for years. The Dong With A Luminous Nose, The Jumblies, The Owl and the Pussycat, and hundreds of other bits of wonderful nonsense. 214 limericks, 3 sets of Nonsense Botany, 5 Nonsense Alphabets, 546 drawings by Lear himself, and much more. 320pp. 5⅜ x 8. 20167-8 Paperbound $1.75

THE WIT AND HUMOR OF OSCAR WILDE, *ed. by Alvin Redman*
Wilde at his most brilliant, in 1000 epigrams exposing weaknesses and hypocrisies of "civilized" society. Divided into 49 categories—sin, wealth, women, America, etc.—to aid writers, speakers. Includes excerpts from his trials, books, plays, criticism. Formerly "The Epigrams of Oscar Wilde." Introduction by Vyvyan Holland, Wilde's only living son. Introductory essay by editor. 260pp. 5⅜ x 8.
20602-5 Paperbound $1.50

A CHILD'S PRIMER OF NATURAL HISTORY, *Oliver Herford*
Scarcely an anthology of whimsy and humor has appeared in the last 50 years without a contribution from Oliver Herford. Yet the works from which these examples are drawn have been almost impossible to obtain! Here at last are Herford's improbable definitions of a menagerie of familiar and weird animals, each verse illustrated by the author's own drawings. 24 drawings in 2 colors; 24 additional drawings. vii + 95pp. 6½ x 6. 21647-0 Paperbound $1.00

THE BROWNIES: THEIR BOOK, *Palmer Cox*
The book that made the Brownies a household word. Generations of readers have enjoyed the antics, predicaments and adventures of these jovial sprites, who emerge from the forest at night to play or to come to the aid of a deserving human. Delightful illustrations by the author decorate nearly every page. 24 short verse tales with 266 illustrations. 155pp. 6⅝ x 9¼.
21265-3 Paperbound $1.50

THE PRINCIPLES OF PSYCHOLOGY,
William James

The full long-course, unabridged, of one of the great classics of Western literature and science. Wonderfully lucid descriptions of human mental activity, the stream of thought, consciousness, time perception, memory, imagination, emotions, reason, abnormal phenomena, and similar topics. Original contributions are integrated with the work of such men as Berkeley, Binet, Mills, Darwin, Hume, Kant, Royce, Schopenhauer, Spinoza, Locke, Descartes, Galton, Wundt, Lotze, Herbart, Fechner, and scores of others. All contrasting interpretations of mental phenomena are examined in detail—introspective analysis, philosophical interpretation, and experimental research. "A classic," *Journal of Consulting Psychology.* "The main lines are as valid as ever," *Psychoanalytical Quarterly.* "Standard reading . . . a classic of interpretation," *Psychiatric Quarterly.* 94 illustrations. 1408pp. 5⅜ x 8.
20381-6, 20382-4 Two volume set, paperbound $6.00

VISUAL ILLUSIONS: THEIR CAUSES, CHARACTERISTICS AND APPLICATIONS,
M. Luckiesh

"Seeing is deceiving," asserts the author of this introduction to virtually every type of optical illusion known. The text both describes and explains the principles involved in color illusions, figure-ground, distance illusions, etc. 100 photographs, drawings and diagrams prove how easy it is to fool the sense: circles that aren't round, parallel lines that seem to bend, stationary figures that seem to move as you stare at them — illustration after illustration strains our credulity at what we see. Fascinating book from many points of view, from applications for artists, in camouflage, etc. to the psychology of vision. New introduction by William Ittleson, Dept. of Psychology, Queens College. Index. Bibliography. xxi + 252pp. 5⅜ x 8½. 21530-X Paperbound $1.75

FADS AND FALLACIES IN THE NAME OF SCIENCE,
Martin Gardner

This is the standard account of various cults, quack systems, and delusions which have masqueraded as science: hollow earth fanatics. Reich and orgone sex energy, dianetics, Atlantis, multiple moons, Forteanism, flying saucers, medical fallacies like iridiagnosis, zone therapy, etc. A new chapter has been added on Bridey Murphy, psionics, and other recent manifestations in this field. This is a fair, reasoned appraisal of eccentric theory which provides excellent inoculation against cleverly masked nonsense. "Should be read by everyone, scientist and non-scientist alike," R. T. Birge, Prof. Emeritus of Physics, Univ. of California; Former President, American Physical Society. Index. x + 365pp. 5⅜ x 8. 20394-8 Paperbound $2.00

ILLUSIONS AND DELUSIONS OF THE SUPERNATURAL AND THE OCCULT,
D. H. Rawcliffe

Holds up to rational examination hundreds of persistent delusions including crystal gazing, automatic writing, table turning, mediumistic trances, mental healing, stigmata, lycanthropy, live burial, the Indian Rope Trick, spiritualism, dowsing, telepathy, clairvoyance, ghosts, ESP, etc. The author explains and exposes the mental and physical deceptions involved, making this not only an exposé of supernatural phenomena, but a valuable exposition of characteristic types of abnormal psychology. Originally titled "The Psychology of the Occult." 14 illustrations. Index. 551pp. 5⅜ x 8. 20503-7 Paperbound $3.50

FAIRY TALE COLLECTIONS, *edited by Andrew Lang*
Andrew Lang's fairy tale collections make up the richest shelf-full of traditional children's stories anywhere available. Lang supervised the translation of stories from all over the world—familiar European tales collected by Grimm, animal stories from Negro Africa, myths of primitive Australia, stories from Russia, Hungary, Iceland, Japan, and many other countries. Lang's selection of translations are unusually high; many authorities consider that the most familiar tales find their best versions in these volumes. All collections are richly decorated and illustrated by H. J. Ford and other artists.

THE BLUE FAIRY BOOK. 37 stories. 138 illustrations. ix + 390pp. 5⅜ x 8½.
21437-0 Paperbound $1.95

THE GREEN FAIRY BOOK. 42 stories. 100 illustrations. xiii + 366pp. 5⅜ x 8½.
21439-7 Paperbound $2.00

THE BROWN FAIRY BOOK. 32 stories. 50 illustrations, 8 in color. xii + 350pp. 5⅜ x 8½.
21438-9 Paperbound $1.95

THE BEST TALES OF HOFFMANN, *edited by E. F. Bleiler*
10 stories by E. T. A. Hoffmann, one of the greatest of all writers of fantasy. The tales include "The Golden Flower Pot," "Automata," "A New Year's Eve Adventure," "Nutcracker and the King of Mice," "Sand-Man," and others. Vigorous characterizations of highly eccentric personalities, remarkably imaginative situations, and intensely fast pacing has made these tales popular all over the world for 150 years. Editor's introduction. 7 drawings by Hoffmann. xxxiii + 419pp. 5⅜ x 8½.
21793-0 Paperbound $2.25

GHOST AND HORROR STORIES OF AMBROSE BIERCE,
edited by E. F. Bleiler
Morbid, eerie, horrifying tales of possessed poets, shabby aristocrats, revived corpses, and haunted malefactors. Widely acknowledged as the best of their kind between Poe and the moderns, reflecting their author's inner torment and bitter view of life. Includes "Damned Thing," "The Middle Toe of the Right Foot," "The Eyes of the Panther," "Visions of the Night," "Moxon's Master," and over a dozen others. Editor's introduction. xxii + 199pp. 5⅜ x 8½.
20767-6 Paperbound $1.50

THREE GOTHIC NOVELS, *edited by E. F. Bleiler*
Originators of the still popular Gothic novel form, influential in ushering in early 19th-century Romanticism. Horace Walpole's *Castle of Otranto*, William Beckford's *Vathek*, John Polidori's *The Vampyre*, and a *Fragment* by Lord Byron are enjoyable as exciting reading or as documents in the history of English literature. Editor's introduction. xi + 291pp. 5⅜ x 8½.
21232-7 Paperbound $2.00

BEST GHOST STORIES OF LEFANU, *edited by E. F. Bleiler*
Though admired by such critics as V. S. Pritchett, Charles Dickens and Henry James, ghost stories by the Irish novelist Joseph Sheridan LeFanu have never become as widely known as his detective fiction. About half of the 16 stories in this collection have never before been available in America. Collection includes "Carmilla" (perhaps the best vampire story ever written), "The Haunted Baronet," "The Fortunes of Sir Robert Ardagh," and the classic "Green Tea." Editor's introduction. 7 contemporary illustrations. Portrait of LeFanu. xii + 467pp. 5⅜ x 8.
20415-4 Paperbound $2.50

EASY-TO-DO ENTERTAINMENTS AND DIVERSIONS WITH COINS, CARDS, STRING, PAPER AND MATCHES, *R. M. Abraham*

Over 300 tricks, games and puzzles will provide young readers with absorbing fun. Sections on card games; paper-folding; tricks with coins, matches and pieces of string; games for the agile; toy-making from common household objects; mathematical recreations; and 50 miscellaneous pastimes. Anyone in charge of groups of youngsters, including hard-pressed parents, and in need of suggestions on how to keep children sensibly amused and quietly content will find this book indispensable. Clear, simple text, copious number of delightful line drawings and illustrative diagrams. Originally titled "Winter Nights' Entertainments." Introduction by Lord Baden Powell. 329 illustrations. v + 186pp. 5⅜ x 8½.   20921-0 Paperbound $1.25

AN INTRODUCTION TO CHESS MOVES AND TACTICS SIMPLY EXPLAINED, *Leonard Barden*

Beginner's introduction to the royal game. Names, possible moves of the pieces, definitions of essential terms, how games are won, etc. explained in 30-odd pages. With this background you'll be able to sit right down and play. Balance of book teaches strategy — openings, middle game, typical endgame play, and suggestions for improving your game. A sample game is fully analyzed. True middle-level introduction, teaching you all the essentials without oversimplifying or losing you in a maze of detail. 58 figures. 102pp. 5⅜ x 8½.   21210-6 Paperbound $1.25

LASKER'S MANUAL OF CHESS, *Dr. Emanuel Lasker*

Probably the greatest chess player of modern times, Dr. Emanuel Lasker held the world championship 28 years, independent of passing schools or fashions. This unmatched study of the game, chiefly for intermediate to skilled players, analyzes basic methods, combinations, position play, the aesthetics of chess, dozens of different openings, etc., with constant reference to great modern games. Contains a brilliant exposition of Steinitz's important theories. Introduction by Fred Reinfeld. Tables of Lasker's tournament record. 3 indices. 308 diagrams. 1 photograph. xxx + 349pp. 5⅜ x 8.20640-8 Paperbound $2.50

COMBINATIONS: THE HEART OF CHESS, *Irving Chernev*

Step-by-step from simple combinations to complex, this book, by a well-known chess writer, shows you the intricacies of pins, counter-pins, knight forks, and smothered mates. Other chapters show alternate lines of play to those taken in actual championship games; boomerang combinations; classic examples of brilliant combination play by Nimzovich, Rubinstein, Tarrasch, Botvinnik, Alekhine and Capablanca. Index. 356 diagrams. ix + 245pp. 5⅜ x 8½.   21744-2 Paperbound $2.00

HOW TO SOLVE CHESS PROBLEMS, *K. S. Howard*

Full of practical suggestions for the fan or the beginner — who knows only the moves of the chessmen. Contains preliminary section and 58 two-move, 46 three-move, and 8 four-move problems composed by 27 outstanding American problem creators in the last 30 years. Explanation of all terms and exhaustive index. "Just what is wanted for the student," Brian Harley. 112 problems, solutions. vi + 171pp. 5⅜ x 8.   20748-X Paperbound $1.50

SOCIAL THOUGHT FROM LORE TO SCIENCE,
H. E. Barnes and H. Becker
An immense survey of sociological thought and ways of viewing, studying, planning, and reforming society from earliest times to the present. Includes thought on society of preliterate peoples, ancient non-Western cultures, and every great movement in Europe, America, and modern Japan. Analyzes hundreds of great thinkers: Plato, Augustine, Bodin, Vico, Montesquieu, Herder, Comte, Marx, etc. Weighs the contributions of utopians, sophists, fascists and communists; economists, jurists, philosophers, ecclesiastics, and every 19th and 20th century school of scientific sociology, anthropology, and social psychology throughout the world. Combines topical, chronological, and regional approaches, treating the evolution of social thought as a process rather than as a series of mere topics. "Impressive accuracy, competence, and discrimination . . . easily the best single survey," *Nation*. Thoroughly revised, with new material up to 1960. 2 indexes. Over 2200 bibliographical notes. Three volume set. Total of 1586pp. 5⅜ x 8.

20901-6, 20902-4, 20903-2 Three volume set, paperbound $10.50

A HISTORY OF HISTORICAL WRITING, *Harry Elmer Barnes*
Virtually the only adequate survey of the whole course of historical writing in a single volume. Surveys developments from the beginnings of historiography in the ancient Near East and the Classical World, up through the Cold War. Covers major historians in detail, shows interrelationship with cultural background, makes clear individual contributions, evaluates and estimates importance; also enormously rich upon minor authors and thinkers who are usually passed over. Packed with scholarship and learning, clear, easily written. Indispensable to every student of history. Revised and enlarged up to 1961. Index and bibliography. xv + 442pp. 5⅜ x 8½.

20104-X Paperbound $3.00

JOHANN SEBASTIAN BACH, *Philipp Spitta*
The complete and unabridged text of the definitive study of Bach. Written some 70 years ago, it is still unsurpassed for its coverage of nearly all aspects of Bach's life and work. There could hardly be a finer non-technical introduction to Bach's music than the detailed, lucid analyses which Spitta provides for hundreds of individual pieces. 26 solid pages are devoted to the B minor mass, for example, and 30 pages to the glorious St. Matthew Passion. This monumental set also includes a major analysis of the music of the 18th century: Buxtehude, Pachelbel, etc. "Unchallenged as the last word on one of the supreme geniuses of music," John Barkham, *Saturday Review Syndicate*. Total of 1819pp. Heavy cloth binding. 5⅜ x 8.

22278-0, 22279-9 Two volume set, clothbound $15.00

BEETHOVEN AND HIS NINE SYMPHONIES, *George Grove*
In this modern middle-level classic of musicology Grove not only analyzes all nine of Beethoven's symphonies very thoroughly in terms of their musical structure, but also discusses the circumstances under which they were written, Beethoven's stylistic development, and much other background material. This is an extremely rich book, yet very easily followed; it is highly recommended to anyone seriously interested in music. Over 250 musical passages. Index. viii + 407pp. 5⅜ x 8.

20334-4 Paperbound $2.50

THE TIME STREAM
John Taine
Acknowledged by many as the best SF writer of the 1920's, Taine (under the name Eric Temple Bell) was also a Professor of Mathematics of considerable renown. Reprinted here are *The Time Stream*, generally considered Taine's best, *The Greatest Game*, a biological-fiction novel, and *The Purple Sapphire*, involving a supercivilization of the past. Taine's stories tie fantastic narratives to frameworks of original and logical scientific concepts. Speculation is often profound on such questions as the nature of time, concept of entropy, cyclical universes, etc. 4 contemporary illustrations. v + 532pp. 5⅜ x 8⅜.

21180-0 Paperbound $3.00

SEVEN SCIENCE FICTION NOVELS,
H. G. Wells
Full unabridged texts of 7 science-fiction novels of the master. Ranging from biology, physics, chemistry, astronomy, to sociology and other studies, Mr. Wells extrapolates whole worlds of strange and intriguing character. "One will have to go far to match this for entertainment, excitement, and sheer pleasure . . ."*New York Times*. Contents: The Time Machine, The Island of Dr. Moreau, The First Men in the Moon, The Invisible Man, The War of the Worlds, The Food of the Gods, In The Days of the Comet. 1015pp. 5⅜ x 8.

20264-X Clothbound $5.00

28 SCIENCE FICTION STORIES OF H. G. WELLS.
Two full, unabridged novels, *Men Like Gods* and *Star Begotten*, plus 26 short stories by the master science-fiction writer of all time! Stories of space, time, invention, exploration, futuristic adventure. Partial contents: *The Country of the Blind, In the Abyss, The Crystal Egg, The Man Who Could Work Miracles, A Story of Days to Come, The Empire of the Ants, The Magic Shop, The Valley of the Spiders, A Story of the Stone Age, Under the Knife, Sea Raiders*, etc. An indispensable collection for the library of anyone interested in science fiction adventure. 928pp. 5⅜ x 8.

20265-8 Clothbound $5.00

THREE MARTIAN NOVELS,
Edgar Rice Burroughs
Complete, unabridged reprinting, in one volume, of Thuvia, Maid of Mars; Chessmen of Mars; The Master Mind of Mars. Hours of science-fiction adventure by a modern master storyteller. Reset in large clear type for easy reading. 16 illustrations by J. Allen St. John. vi + 490pp. 5⅜ x 8½.

20039-6.Paperbound $2.50

AN INTELLECTUAL AND CULTURAL HISTORY OF THE WESTERN WORLD,
Harry Elmer Barnes
Monumental 3-volume survey of intellectual development of Europe from primitive cultures to the present day. Every significant product of human intellect traced through history: art, literature, mathematics, physical sciences, medicine, music, technology, social sciences, religions, jurisprudence, education, etc. Presentation is lucid and specific, analyzing in detail specific discoveries, theories, literary works, and so on. Revised (1965) by recognized scholars in specialized fields under the direction of Prof. Barnes. Revised bibliography. Indexes. 24 illustrations. Total of xxix + 1318pp.

21275-0, 21276-9, 21277-7 Three volume set, paperbound $7.75

HEAR ME TALKIN' TO YA, *edited by Nat Shapiro and Nat Hentoff*
In their own words, Louis Armstrong, King Oliver, Fletcher Henderson, Bunk
Johnson, Bix Beiderbecke, Billy Holiday, Fats Waller, Jelly Roll Morton,
Duke Ellington, and many others comment on the origins of jazz in New
Orleans and its growth in Chicago's South Side, Kansas City's jam sessions,
Depression Harlem, and the modernism of the West Coast schools. Taken
from taped conversations, letters, magazine articles, other first-hand sources.
Editors' introduction. xvi + 429pp. 5⅜ x 8½.   21726-4 Paperbound $2.50

THE JOURNAL OF HENRY D. THOREAU
A 25-year record by the great American observer and critic, as complete a
record of a great man's inner life as is anywhere available. Thoreau's Journals
served him as raw material for his formal pieces, as a place where he could
develop his ideas, as an outlet for his interests in wild life and plants, in
writing as an art, in classics of literature, Walt Whitman and other contemporaries, in politics, slavery, individual's relation to the State, etc. The
Journals present a portrait of a remarkable man, and are an observant social
history. Unabridged republication of 1906 edition, Bradford Torrey and
Francis H. Allen, editors. Illustrations. Total of 1888pp. 8⅜ x 12¼.
                    20312-3, 20313-1 Two volume set, clothbound $30.00

A SHAKESPEARIAN GRAMMAR, *E. A. Abbott*
Basic reference to Shakespeare and his contemporaries, explaining through
thousands of quotations from Shakespeare, Jonson, Beaumont and Fletcher,
North's *Plutarch* and other sources the grammatical usage differing from the
modern. First published in 1870 and written by a scholar who spent much of
his life isolating principles of Elizabethan language, the book is unlikely ever
to be superseded. Indexes. xxiv + 511pp. 5⅜ x 8½. 21582-2 Paperbound $3.00

FOLK-LORE OF SHAKESPEARE, *T. F. Thistelton Dyer*
Classic study, drawing from Shakespeare a large body of references to supernatural beliefs, terminology of falconry and hunting, games and sports, good
luck charms, marriage customs, folk medicines, superstitions about plants,
animals, birds, argot of the underworld, sexual slang of London, proverbs,
drinking customs, weather lore, and much else. From full compilation comes
a mirror of the 17th-century popular mind. Index. ix + 526pp. 5⅜ x 8½.
                              21614-4 Paperbound $3.25

THE NEW VARIORUM SHAKESPEARE, *edited by H. H. Furness*
By far the richest editions of the plays ever produced in any country or
language. Each volume contains complete text (usually First Folio) of the
play, all variants in Quarto and other Folio texts, editorial changes by every
major editor to Furness's own time (1900), footnotes to obscure references or
language, extensive quotes from literature of Shakespearian criticism, essays
on plot sources (often reprinting sources in full), and much more.

HAMLET, *edited by H. H. Furness*
Total of xxvi + 905pp. 5⅜ x 8½.
                    21004-9, 21005-7 Two volume set, paperbound $5.50

TWELFTH NIGHT, *edited by H. H. Furness*
Index. xxii + 434pp. 5⅜ x 8½.   21189-4 Paperbound $2.75

LA BOHEME BY GIACOMO PUCCINI,
translated and introduced by Ellen H. Bleiler
Complete handbook for the operagoer, with everything needed for full enjoy-
ment except the musical score itself. Complete Italian libretto, with new,
modern English line-by-line translation—the only libretto printing all repeats;
biography of Puccini; the librettists; background to the opera, Murger's La
Boheme, etc.; circumstances of composition and performances; plot summary;
and pictorial section of 73 illustrations showing Puccini, famous singers and
performances, etc. Large clear type for easy reading. 124pp. 5⅜ x 8½.
20404-9 Paperbound $1.50

ANTONIO STRADIVARI: HIS LIFE AND WORK (1644-1737),
W. Henry Hill, Arthur F. Hill, and Alfred E. Hill
Still the only book that really delves into life and art of the incomparable
Italian craftsman, maker of the finest musical instruments in the world today.
The authors, expert violin-makers themselves, discuss Stradivari's ancestry, his
construction and finishing techniques, distinguished characteristics of many
of his instruments and their locations. Included, too, is story of introduction
of his instruments into France, England, first revelation of their supreme
merit, and information on his labels, number of instruments made, prices,
mystery of ingredients of his varnish, tone of pre-1684 Stradivari violin and
changes between 1684 and 1690. An extremely interesting, informative account
for all music lovers, from craftsman to concert-goer. Republication of original
(1902) edition. New introduction by Sydney Beck, Head of Rare Book and
Manuscript Collections, Music Division, New York Public Library. Analytical
index by Rembert Wurlitzer. Appendixes. 68 illustrations. 30 full-page plates.
4 in color. xxvi + 315pp. 5⅜ x 8½. 20425-1 Paperbound $3.00

MUSICAL AUTOGRAPHS FROM MONTEVERDI TO HINDEMITH,
Emanuel Winternitz
For beauty, for intrinsic interest, for perspective on the composer's personality,
for subtleties of phrasing, shading, emphasis indicated in the autograph but
suppressed in the printed score, the mss. of musical composition are fascinating
documents which repay close study in many different ways. This 2-volume
work reprints facsimiles of mss. by virtually every major composer, and many
minor figures—196 examples in all. A full text points out what can be learned
from mss., analyzes each sample. Index. Bibliography. 18 figures. 196 plates.
Total of 170pp. of text. 7⅞ x 10¾.
21312-9, 21313-7 Two volume set, paperbound $5.00

J. S. BACH,
Albert Schweitzer
One of the few great full-length studies of Bach's life and work, and the
study upon which Schweitzer's renown as a musicologist rests. On first appearance (1911), revolutionized Bach performance. The only writer on Bach to
be musicologist, performing musician, and student of history, theology and
philosophy, Schweitzer contributes particularly full sections on history of German Protestant church music, theories on motivic pictorial representations
in vocal music, and practical suggestions for performance. Translated by
Ernest Newman. Indexes. 5 illustrations. 650 musical examples. Total of xix
+ 928pp. 5⅜ x 8½. 21631-4, 21632-2 Two volume set, paperbound $5.00

THE METHODS OF ETHICS, *Henry Sidgwick*
Propounding no organized system of its own, study subjects every major methodological approach to ethics to rigorous, objective analysis. Study discusses and relates ethical thought of Plato, Aristotle, Bentham, Clarke, Butler, Hobbes, Hume, Mill, Spencer, Kant, and dozens of others. Sidgwick retains conclusions from each system which follow from ethical premises, rejecting the faulty. Considered by many in the field to be among the most important treatises on ethical philosophy. Appendix. Index. xlvii + 528pp. 5⅜ x 8½.
21608-X Paperbound $3.00

TEUTONIC MYTHOLOGY, *Jakob Grimm*
A milestone in Western culture; the work which established on a modern basis the study of history of religions and comparative religions. 4-volume work assembles and interprets everything available on religious and folkloristic beliefs of Germanic people (including Scandinavians, Anglo-Saxons, etc.). Assembling material from such sources as Tacitus, surviving Old Norse and Icelandic texts, archeological remains, folktales, surviving superstitions, comparative traditions, linguistic analysis, etc. Grimm explores pagan deities, heroes, folklore of nature, religious practices, and every other area of pagan German belief. To this day, the unrivaled, definitive, exhaustive study. Translated by J. S. Stallybrass from 4th (1883) German edition. Indexes. Total of lxxvii + 1887pp. 5⅜ x 8½.
21602-0, 21603-9, 21604-7, 21605-5 Four volume set, paperbound $12.00

THE I CHING, *translated by James Legge*
Called "The Book of Changes" in English, this is one of the Five Classics edited by Confucius, basic and central to Chinese thought. Explains perhaps the most complex system of divination known, founded on the theory that all things happening at any one time have characteristic features which can be isolated and related. Significant in Oriental studies, in history of religions and philosophy, and also to Jungian psychoanalysis and other areas of modern European thought. Index. Appendixes. 6 plates. xxi + 448pp. 5⅜ x 8½.
21062-6 Paperbound $2.75

HISTORY OF ANCIENT PHILOSOPHY, *W. Windelband*
One of the clearest, most accurate comprehensive surveys of Greek and Roman philosophy. Discusses ancient philosophy in general, intellectual life in Greece in the 7th and 6th centuries B.C., Thales, Anaximander, Anaximenes, Heraclitus, the Eleatics, Empedocles, Anaxagoras, Leucippus, the Pythagoreans, the Sophists, Socrates, Democritus (20 pages), Plato (50 pages), Aristotle (70 pages), the Peripatetics, Stoics, Epicureans, Sceptics, Neo-platonists, Christian Apologists, etc. 2nd German edition translated by H. E. Cushman. xv + 393pp. 5⅜ x 8.
20357-3 Paperbound $3.00

THE PALACE OF PLEASURE, *William Painter*
Elizabethan versions of Italian and French novels from *The Decameron*, Cinthio, Straparola, Queen Margaret of Navarre, and other continental sources — the very work that provided Shakespeare and dozens of his contemporaries with many of their plots and sub-plots and, therefore, justly considered one of the most influential books in all English literature. It is also a book that any reader will still enjoy. Total of cviii + 1,224pp.
21691-8, 21692-6, 21693-4 Three volume set, paperbound $8.25

THE WONDERFUL WIZARD OF OZ, *L. F. Baum*
All the original W. W. Denslow illustrations in full color—as much a part of
"The Wizard" as Tenniel's drawings are of "Alice in Wonderland." "The
Wizard" is still America's best-loved fairy tale, in which, as the author expresses
it, "The wonderment and joy are retained and the heartaches and nightmares
left out." Now today's young readers can enjoy every word and wonderful picture of the original book. New introduction by Martin Gardner. A Baum
bibliography. 23 full-page color plates. viii + 268pp. 5⅜ x 8.
20691-2 Paperbound $1.95

THE MARVELOUS LAND OF OZ, *L. F. Baum*
This is the equally enchanting sequel to the "Wizard," continuing the adventures of the Scarecrow and the Tin Woodman. The hero this time is a little
boy named Tip, and all the delightful Oz magic is still present. This is the
Oz book with the Animated Saw-Horse, the Woggle-Bug, and Jack Pumpkin-
head. All the original John R. Neill illustrations, 10 in full color. 287pp.
5⅜ x 8. 20692-0 Paperbound $1.75

ALICE'S ADVENTURES UNDER GROUND, *Lewis Carroll*
The original *Alice in Wonderland*, hand-lettered and illustrated by Carroll
himself, and originally presented as a Christmas gift to a child-friend. Adults
as well as children will enjoy this charming volume, reproduced faithfully
in this Dover edition. While the story is essentially the same, there are slight
changes, and Carroll's spritely drawings present an intriguing alternative to
the famous Tenniel illustrations. One of the most popular books in Dover's
catalogue. Introduction by Martin Gardner. 38 illustrations. 128pp. 5⅜ x 8½.
21482-6 Paperbound $1.00

THE NURSERY "ALICE," *Lewis Carroll*
While most of us consider *Alice in Wonderland* a story for children of all
ages, Carroll himself felt it was beyond younger children. He therefore provided this simplified version, illustrated with the famous Tenniel drawings
enlarged and colored in delicate tints, for children aged "from Nought to
Five." Dover's edition of this now rare classic is a faithful copy of the 1889
printing, including 20 illustrations by Tenniel, and front and back covers
reproduced in full color. Introduction by Martin Gardner. xxiii + 67pp.
6⅛ x 9¼. 21610-1 Paperbound $1.75

THE STORY OF KING ARTHUR AND HIS KNIGHTS, *Howard Pyle*
A fast-paced, exciting retelling of the best known Arthurian legends for young
readers by one of America's best story tellers and illustrators. The sword
Excalibur, wooing of Guinevere, Merlin and his downfall, adventures of Sir
Pellias and Gawaine, and others. The pen and ink illustrations are vividly
imagined and wonderfully drawn. 41 illustrations. xviii + 313pp. 6⅛ x 9¼.
21445-1 Paperbound $2.00

Prices subject to change without notice.

Available at your book dealer or write for free catalogue to Dept. Adsci,
Dover Publications, Inc., 180 Varick St., N.Y., N.Y. 10014. Dover publishes more
than 150 books each year on science, elementary and advanced mathematics,
biology, music, art, literary history, social sciences and other areas.